W9-AOA-884

ON AIR

ALSO BY TAVIS SMILEY

JUST A THOUGHT
HARD LEFT

ON AIR

THE BEST OF TAVIS SMILEY ON THE TOM JOYNER MORNING SHOW

THOUGHTS ON CULTURE, POLITICS & RACE

INTRODUCTION BY
TOM JOYNER

TAVIS SMILEY

PINES ONE PUBLICATIONS
LOS ANGELES

Publisher's Note

This publication contains adaptations of commentaries originally heard on the *Tom Joyner Morning Show.* Many of the commentaries include pieces of public information taken from various newspapers, periodicals and books. It is sold with the understanding that the author provided accurate and authoritative information with regard to the subject matter covered.

Books are available to organizations, corporations and professional associations at quantity discounts. For information, contact the sales department at Pines One Publications (213) 290-1182; Fax (213) 295-3880; or e-mail pinesone@worldnet.att.net

Cover and text design by Laurie Williams/A Street Called Straight
Back cover background photo by Sammy Davis

Publisher's Cataloging-in-Publication Data

Smiley, Tavis
On air : the best of Tavis Smiley on the Tom Joyner morning show / Tavis Smiley. —1st ed.
p. cm.
Preassigned LCCN: 97-76052
ISBN: 1-890194-33-6

1. United States—Race relations. 2. Afro-Americans—Racial Identity. 3. United States—Politics and government—1993- I. Title

E185.S65 1998 305.8'00973
QBI98-169

Pines One Publications 3870 Crenshaw Blvd., Suite 931,
Los Angeles, CA 90008
http://www.pinesone.com

Printed in the United States of America
10 9 8 7 6 5 4 3 2

FIRST EDITION

For
"Big Momma"
Daisy M. Robinson

and

for the *Tom Joyner Morning Show*
audience

Thanks for listening to me
on air!

Contents

Acknowledgements

Faith. Family. Friends. These are the things that sustain us.

First and foremost, God. As the old gospel hymn declares, "Without Him, I would be nothing. Without Him, I would fail. Without Him, I would be drifting like a ship without a sail."

Next, I acknowledge my family by name as I do in each book. One, because I love them. And two, because I want to remain loved by them! Much love to my parents, Emory G. Smiley and Joyce M. Smiley, and my nine siblings: Pam, Phyllis, Garnie, Paul, Patrick, Maury, Derwin, Scooter and Dion.

Now, here's where it gets tough because I have more friends than I have space. Fortunately, in books past I have had the chance to mention them by name as well. You remain loyal friends and you know who you are.

To the "Fly Jock" Tom Joyner, I love you man! To Sybil Wilkes, I'd love to love you! To J. Anthony Brown, I love your Momma! To Miss Dupree, I love you for sharing "the gift" with me. To Myra J., I love your bald head! To George Wallace, I love your stand-up and I really love the God in you. To Melvin...can I say I love Melvin without getting into trouble? Oh well, I love you Melvin! Ta! Ta! To Mary Boyce, I love your quiet genius.

And now to the *really* important people at the *Tom Joyner Morning Show*: Yolanda Starks, I love you for just getting it done–no excuses. Cleo "Dr Rock" Turner. I love your Style. Ross Alan, without you there would be no *ON AIR*. David Starr or whatever your name is, I'd love it if you would returned my calls!! LaDor Frank, I love you for loving Tom! Tom Joyner, Jr., I love you for honoring your Dad.

And finally, to my publisher and abiding friend Denise Pines, where do we go from here? Up baby, up!

Introduction

I first met Tavis Smiley a few years ago at a White House conference aimed at getting the Black media more involved in the Clinton/Gore re-election campaign. The thing I remember most about that day was the inspiring and enlightening words from the late Ron Brown. The Commerce Secretary asked a room full of members of the Black press to turn off their microphones and to put down their pens and pads. He said he wanted to take a moment to be "real with us." Then he said, "Those Republicans are some mean sons of b------." When I later learned that Tavis was tight with Ron Brown, and Ron Brown was that "down," I knew Tavis was my kind of journalist. After reading his book, *Hard Left*, I was even more sure.

It was around this same period that I was trying to come up with a way to center a voter registration campaign around the *Tom Joyner Morning Show*. With about five million African American listeners tuning into our show five days a week, I felt we had a duty to get people to the polls in November. But I wanted to do more than a series of public announcements from celebrities urging people to turn out to vote. Admittedly, the idea I did come up with was a little "out there," but it was still better than a thirty-second message from Bobby Brown telling folks why voting is their civic duty. I wanted to take a 1996 Lexus to each of the 95+ cities where our show is heard, register people to vote and give each person who registered a chance to win the Lexus, complete with a gold kit, of course. Hey, some precincts offer voters coffee and donuts...what's wrong with a Lexus? When I brought the idea to Tavis, he said, "Hold up, Fly Jock, I think there could be some problems with your plan, but how about this..." Tavis suggested voter education, pure and simple. He said voter education was crucial and needed to go hand in hand with voter registration. I still liked my Lexus idea, but I liked Tavis's idea even better. And we ran with it.

Tavis did daily commentaries on our shows that gave the audience, and the *Tom Joyner Morning Show* crew, invaluable lessons in politics from an African American perspective. And the beauty of it was that he did this in about three minutes. He was an instant hit. The phones lit up with questions from average, ordinary people. They wanted to know things like "How do I know where to register to vote?" and "Can I vote if I've been to jail?" We knew we'd hit a hot button. There were thousands of people out there who didn't vote just because they had never really understood why they should vote, until Tavis broke it down for them. And that's what Tavis does best. He brings the message home.

After a few weeks of Tavis's daily commentaries, the *Tom Joyner Morning Show* hit the road with a voter registration campaign that we called "Partying with a Purpose." We headed for Chicago, St. Louis, D.C., Philly, Dallas and Atlanta. Each stop included a live concert featuring acts such as The Gap Band, the Chi-Lites, ConFunkShun, and Ann Nesby. The price of admission was your voter registration card. If you didn't have one, there were people to register you right on the spot. Tavis mapped out our road tour to include cities where positions of African American politicians were at stake. For example, in Atlanta, Democratic Congresswoman Cynthia McKinney was in big trouble because of redistricting. By the time they were done redrawing the lines, her majority Black district had been drastically reduced. I think she was the only Black person left! I know our registration campaign played a large part in her re-election. And it was Tavis who drove home the point so well, that people were compelled not to just register, but to cast their ballots when November rolled around. He got people fired up about voting, and if you don't believe me, ask MTV. Tavis suggested that we give out their "Rock the Vote" 1-800 number to allow people to register over the phone. Our listeners blew their system out! Of course, some of them were calling to request music, but that's another story.

Tavis's daily dose of political commentary was such a success that we knew we needed to keep him around. So now he joins the rest of us two days a week on the *Tom Joyner Morning Show* from a studio in Washington D.C. and he has become a regular member of our crew. He also travels with us when we're on the road as often as his busy schedule will allow. In fact, when he isn't with us, we spend half our time explaining his absence to the female members of our live audiences. Oh, yes, Tavis has groupies. He's a rock star that doesn't play an instrument, an athlete who doesn't run touchdowns or slam-dunk, a movie star who never had a starring role on the big screen. Am I jealous? A little, but it's great to see a young Black male be heralded, not because he has platinum records or a sneaker endorsement, but because he's a smart brother who knows his stuff. It's also great because since he has so many women after him, he lets me have a crack at the overflow.

I realized just how valuable Tavis was to our staff when he accompanied us to South Africa in the spring of 1997. We had the honor and privilege of broadcasting a week of shows live from the MotherLand. As we made preparations for the broadcast, we recognized that we needed to: (a) bring someone along who was knowledgeable about the country and its politics, and (b) bring someone smart enough to keep our newsperson, Sybil Wilkes, engaged in conversation during a thirteen-hour airplane ride. Who else could fill the bill but Tavis? His keen insight and general knowledge were just the spices we needed as we brought our listeners the flavor of our South African journey. It was Tavis who reminded us all how the new-found freedom our African brothers and sisters enjoyed since the fall of apartheid was so similar to what most Black Americans experienced after our civil rights victories in the 1960s. Now thirty some odd years later, we see those victories being challenged at every turn. As we witness the ban of affirmative action in California, and possibly twenty-six other states, Tavis wondered whether the Black South Africans would be faced with the same challenges in a few decades. Would they too take their rights for granted? Would they have to be begged to go to the polls at election time? Would they be naïve enough to think that a conservative government would not turn back the clock on civil rights?

Tavis was just as outspoken in South Africa as he is anywhere else. When the common-law wife of Steven Biko told our audience that harboring ill-will against those who oppressed them under the system of apartheid was nonproductive and a waste of their energy, we all listened intently. Most of us began to go along with her way of thinking because we figured, hey, she lived through it, and if she thinks they should be forgiven, who are we to disagree? But Tavis wasn't going for it. He respectfully told her that he understood that no gain could come from dwelling on the past and that the present and future of Blacks in South Africa was the most important thing now. But still, he said, someone needs to pay! That's our Tavis.

I only remember one instance when Tavis's outspokenness got him into a little trouble. We were on air discussing the infidelities of President Clinton's political consultant Dick Morris. Morris got busted when a woman he was seeing claimed he had revealed White House secrets to her. On air, Tavis referred to the woman as a "ho'" . I stopped him mid-sentence and said, "Tavis, Tavis, we can't say "ho'" on our show." "Well, that's what she was," he said, and continued on with his commentary. That's one he'll never live down...we still have it on tape.

Tavis's politics go beyond what's happening on Capitol Hill or down the street inside the White House. When *Fox* TV announced that the number one and number two most-watched television programs by African Americans would not be on their fall schedule, Tavis went to work. He was outraged, not because he was necessarily a huge fan of *Living Single* and *New York Undercover*, but because *Fox* had the audacity to insult its Black audience by canceling our favorite programs. When he enlisted our help to try to save these *Fox* programs, I was leery. We had previously tried unsuccessfully to keep *Roc*, also a *Fox* show, and *Under One Roof* at *CBS* on air by urging our audience to write those networks. "They don't listen to us," I said. But when Tavis said, "No network would ever consider canceling *Friends* or *Seinfeld*, two of the most-watched television shows by White America." Not only did I agree to let him get the message out on our show, I wrote a letter to *Fox* myself. Again, Tavis broke it down! And not only did *Fox* return *Living Single* to its time slot in September 1997, the President of *Fox*, Peter Roth, announced the series's return on our show. Our listeners had flooded *Fox* with letters, faxes and e-mail.

Tavis's tireless search for truth and justice sometimes lands him and us in the most unlikely of places. When he learned that the very high-brow Christie's auction house in New York would be including slavery artifacts as a part of its Civil War era auction, Tavis cried out— "Foul play!"

He gave our audience the phone number to Christie's at 8:30 a.m. and by 9:30 a.m. Christie's announced it had removed the slavery era items from its sale. The president of Christie's, Patricia Hambrecht, who later came on our program, said, "Hey, we pulled up! Don't go Nat Turner on us!"

Whether Tavis is with us on the road to St. Louis or South Africa, there are two things we can always count on from him, stimulating conversation and bad jokes. Just like the singer who wants to act, and the athlete who longs to rap, Tavis desperately wants to be a stand-up comedian, and with our crew who includes J. Anthony Brown, George Wallace, Myra J. and Miss Dupree, Tavis is way out of his league. It doesn't stop him from trying though, and you've got to love his persistence.

If I'm the "hardest working man in radio," Tavis is the hardest working political commentator... and the most talkative. And since he talks fast, he has more time to get more words in. He can say more intelligent things in three minutes than most people can say in thirty. I'm just afraid he's going to blow out his voice box.

Tavis has become a household name on our show. Well, sometimes it's Tavis, sometimes it's T*r*avis. Even when people mispronounce his name, it's to give him a compliment. We tease him that since he came from such a large family, by the time his parents got to him they had run out of names, and his response is, "Just spell it right on the check, player." I'm glad to do it because he helps us accomplish the primary goal of our show, which is to entertain and inform our listeners daily.

We're very lucky to have Tavis as a part of our crew, and even more lucky are the millions who tune in to get their "politics on" two days a week. Like me, they've grown to trust and respect this brother. I can almost hear them saying along with me after every commentary, "Break it down, Tavis, break it down."

Tom Joyner
March 1998
Dallas, Texas

REFLECTIONS

January 14, 1997

Tom Joyner Morning Show Topic: Medal of Honor for Black Soldiers

Yesterday at the White House there were seven Black soldiers who were cited for bravery and valor. Mr. Vernon Baker of Idaho was the only soldier who was actually present yesterday and that's because these Black soldiers were being cited for their gallantry in World War II, if you can believe it. Although there were 1.2 million Black Americans who served in the military during World War II, until yesterday not a single African American had ever received the nation's highest military award for service during World War II—the Medal of Honor. President Clinton changed that yesterday for seven African Americans—six posthumously were honored for their bravery and for their service during World War II. In addition to veteran Vernon Baker, the descendants of the other six honorees were present at the White House yesterday.

One can understand (not to be confused with accept) how the racial climate back in the day would have prevented those brothers from getting the respect they deserved. As I watched this ceremony yesterday, it made me as angry as it did proud. And at the same time, it raised more issues than it resolved. Not the least of these is why in the heck it took so long. This war was a half of a century ago, and one has to ask what's been happening all of these years that it just now comes to be that these African Americans are being awarded this Medal of Honor for their bravery. It may not have happened in five, ten or twenty years, but why it took a half of a century for these brothers to finally get the respect that they deserved is an enigma to me. And what's really ironic about all of this is that even today there are more African Americans proportionately who serve in the armed forces than there are White Americans or anyone else. Yet, African Americans, and particularly African American men, are often port rayed as unpatriotic.

It makes absolutely no sense. I mean, if putting your life on the line for your country doesn't qualify you as a patriot, what does? You get the conservatives and those on the Right who always talk about faith, family and freedom, and somehow we are portrayed as the odd men out. Yet, more of us put our lives on the line for our country than anyone else, and still we are deemed and viewed as being unpatriotic African Americans. I thought it was awfully fitting that even though it took a half of a century to get there, finally we saw some African Americans being honored for their service during World War II.

This all started with a study on Blacks and World War II initiated by Shaw University (a historically Black college in North Carolina) and military historians in 1993, commissioned then by Secretary of the Army John Shannon. One of the things the study revealed is that Black soldiers were not given a chance to really participate in the front lines as other soldiers, in part, because they were believed to be genetically inferior, afraid of the dark, and frightened of engaging the enemy. If yesterday's ceremony doesn't prove how ridiculous this notion is, what does?

Mr. Shannon deserves some props for finally getting the study underway. This story underscores something I keep coming back to, and will throughout the year about African Americans getting involved. It took a Black university to get this ceremony to take place yesterday. If we don't get involved, if we don't tell our own story, you know it's going to be "his" story as opposed to "our" story. Shaw University deserves great respect for being there at the center of this effort and making this ceremony come to fruition.

Afraid of the dark? Imagine that. If we haven't lived in the dark long enough and succeeded, I don't know who has.

February 13, 1997

TJMS Topic: O.J., One Last Time

Here are the last of my observations on the O.J. matter.

Let me start with Fred Goldman's startling offer to O.J. yesterday. He said he didn't want any money. He wanted O.J. to sign a confession, and he wouldn't take any of the money. Mr. Goldman is about as slick as sandpaper. The fact of the matter is either it is about the money—as Cuba Gooding Jr. said in Jerry McGuire, "Show me the money!" —or it ain't about the money.

All along Goldman's been saying it's not about the money, so if it isn't about the money, then it ain't about money. The money was never contingent upon a confession being signed. So the fact of the matter is that O.J., whether you believe him or not, has maintained his innocence all along. Why would he all of a sudden come around and sign a confession, now that a judgment has been found against him? For that matter, what would he be signing anyway? This is a very shrewd move on Mr. Goldman's part. Again, I think he is about as slick as sandpaper trying to ask somebody to sign something. You know he's not going to sign that, man!

Two, talk about sending a message. Did anybody notice that Daniel Petrocelli said not once, not twice, but about a dozen times in his civil trial closing argument, that he wanted this jury to send a message that double murder would not be tolerated. He wanted this jury to use their common sense (his words) and send a message. Now correct me if I'm wrong. Wasn't Johnnie L. Cochran vilified by White folks and the media for asking the Black jury in the criminal trial to send a message? I haven't heard anyone talk about that.

Three, even the experts were surprised by this jury award. This $25 million plus the $8.5 million is a total of $33.5 million dollars. The plaintiffs got more than what they had asked for. If that isn't sending a message, I don't know what is.

Four, one of the jurors, in fact some of the jurors, intimated or suggested that this wasn't even about a preponderance of the evidence with them. This went way beyond the preponderance of the evidence, in fact, beyond a reasonable doubt standard. One juror said she was 100% certain that he had done it. Again, I think it underscores that we still live in two fundamentally different Americas, one White, the other Black.

My fifth point also illustrates this idea about two different Americas. One juror, the one Black alternate, Mary, saw everything differently than the White jurors who were sitting in this trial. Again, we still live in two different Americas and something has to be done about the most intractable and divisive issue in this country—the issue of race.

Six, the predominately White jury announced in their press conference that they found O.J.'s defense a bit incredulous. They could not believe the defense's theory of police tampering, or police misconduct, or that police sometimes plant evidence. A Black jury, because of their life experiences, see police one way, and White America sees them another way. The White jurors just dismissed the idea, even the remote possibility that sometimes police engage in misconduct. But there are, in fact, some rogue cops on police departments across the country.

Seven, did you hear about the White juror who made the comment that he found Kato Kalin more credible than O.J. Simpson? Talk about an oxymoron! Whoever thought that the word credible and Kato could be used in the same sentence?

Eight, when Juditha Brown, Nicole Brown-Simpson's mother, was asked when she knew that O.J. in fact had killed her daughter, her first response was: "I knew the moment the phone rang." Don't get me started on what that statement means. This is your son-in-law who earlier that day you were seen on a video hugging and kissing. But you knew the moment the phone rang that the guy who has been taking care of you and paying your bills, etc., had killed your daughter? Where were you all this time? But I ain't going to go there.

Nine, I don't know if you know that they're changing the laws in California. They changed the law right after the criminal trial so that diaries could be included as evidence in trials. And there is a proposed law in California to change the existing law so that defendants convicted of liability in murder cases will lose custody of their children. We see politicians in California changing laws around this one case. I mean it is absolutely insane.

Finally, I keep hearing that Black folks are being racist for calling this a White verdict in the civil case. Let me remind everybody that the first jury who was demonized, demeaned, called racist, were the Black folks who sat in the criminal case. Had it not been labeled a Black verdict by the media, there would be no label of a White verdict by others in this country. We need to be clear about that and quit letting them get away with demonizing the first jury and now trying to call African Americans racist who think that this was a White verdict the second time around. If they hadn't done it the first time, it wouldn't have come back the second time. As Malcolm X said, "In some ways, the chickens are coming home to roost."

February 25, 1997

TJMS Topic: Dr. King's Assassination Revisited

I'm talking today about the original Martin. We mentioned last week, Tom, that we were going to talk about this case today, and not just today, but, in fact, until something is done to make sure that this case is reopened. We all know that twenty-nine years ago Dr. Martin Luther King Jr. was assassinated. Some of us at the time were yet unborn, others were babies and some, of course, remember exactly where we were and exactly what we were doing when we heard the tragic news.

Since this is Black History Month, we want everyone to know the history which sadly includes another tragedy. Let me offer a quick review of some of the facts, at least as we know them.

James Earl Ray confessed to the murder of Dr. King, but shortly thereafter, in fact almost immediately, he recanted his confession and has since been seeking a jury trial which he never received for almost thirty years. Because he confessed to the assassination, there was never a jury trial for James

Earl Ray to argue his innocence.

The fact that Ray and his attorneys now want to run some updated scientific tests is at the heart of the case. They want to use a scanning electron microscope to test the high-powered rifle that Mr. Ray allegedly used in order to determine whether or not the bullet that killed Dr. King did in fact come from Ray's weapon.

Last week in Memphis, a judge listened to their case. Ms. Coretta Scott King and Dexter Scott King, the second son, testified at that hearing. They urged the judge to let the case be heard. It seems like a strange alliance: the Kings and the Rays coming together. However, both say they want the truth. Of course, the King family's motivations are somewhat different, I would suspect, from the Ray family's motivations. Regardless, all of this is reaching a crescendo now because James Earl Ray has been diagnosed with cirrhosis of the liver. So the urgency of reopening this case right away, learning whatever it is that Ray knows, and evaluating whatever evidence may come out about what happened is now paramount.

Three decades later, many questions still persist. Not the least of which is what did the FBI know and when did they know it? Was there, in fact, a conspiracy, perhaps involving the United States government?

J. Edgar Hoover, who was the head of the FBI at the time, was no fan of Dr. King. We all know there was wiretapping and scoping out of Dr. King by the FBI. Hoover was no fan of J.F.K. (John F. Kennedy) or R.F.K. (Robert F. Kennedy) either, and all three of them were assassinated. Also, how could Ray, who had been known as a klutz and bungled so many of his crime exploits in the past, pull off such a monumental assassination all by himself? Many still don't believe that this man could have pulled this kind of assassination off alone.

And where did such a poor man get all the money it required to escape from the United States to go to Europe, and to travel for some time before he was finally located? How was he able to finance his travels through Europe just after the assassination?

Those are just some of the questions, but certainly there is a litany of questions that still persist about what happened, and an urgency for opening this case now that Mr. Ray is nearing death. The time could not be more propitious and so you see the King family requesting last week that this case ought to be reopened.

Now we may never know the whole truth, in fact, we may never know all the details of what happened. But reopening this case could shed a lot of light where there has been darkness regarding what happened twenty-nine years ago and at least start to answer some of these questions before Oliver Stone does the movie and just screws everything up.

Afterthought: *While I happen to know and have the greatest respect for the King family, I was disappointed when they publicly stated that they thought James Earl Ray was innocent of this crime. While he may not have acted alone, to declare him "innocent" was, I thought, somewhat näive.*

March 11, 1997

TJMS Topic: Notorious B.I.G.

I want to talk briefly this morning about the murder of rap artist Notorious B.I.G. over the weekend in L.A. First of all, I'm getting sick of all this stuff happening in L.A. It gives my hometown a bad name. We've got to move this crime someplace outside of Los Angeles. On top of that, Willie Williams, the first Black police chief, was turned out of his job yesterday in Los Angeles. He was denied a second five-year term. So now you don't even have a Black Chief of Police to watch your back if you're in L.A..

In any event, the murder of Notorious B.I.G. is going to spin off, in fact already has spun off, a number of predictable, but necessary, conversations in Black America. I suspect for at least a minute or so, we will be talking about things like gangsta rap, the lyric issue, the misogyny issue, and all the other issues related to whether or not gangsta rap is a viable art form.

There will continue to be conversations about this East Coast/West Coast conflict. I tend to think that it really wasn't a whole coast on the East or the entire coast on the West going against one another other. It was more like an individual conflict namely between the two folks who are now dead. Biggie Smalls and Tupac Shakur. I never bought into this whole entire coast against the other coast. I just thought there were two particular camps who were at each other.

And now we know that Tupac and Biggie are both dead. I suspect we'll also continue to have some conversation, although not enough, mostly about the White executives who market, promote and sell this nonsense and haul truckloads of money to the bank, but won't let their own kids listen to this music. Unfortunately, there is not enough conversation about the executives who are making all this money. Those are some of the predictable conversations I think that will dominate this situation.

The discussion I think we ought to be having, but are not hearing enough of, is the Black-on-Black violence issue. In light of Tupac's death six months ago and now Biggie's death, this whole issue of Black-on-Black crime needs to be discussed. Admittedly, there are some folks who raise hell with me everytime I even use the term Black-on-Black crime. Some folks don't like the term because nobody talks about White-on-White crime when White folks kill people. I understand that.

But then again, we are now at the point in Black history where for the first time more African Americans have killed African Americans than the Klan ever killed in all their ugly and sick years of existence. We have wiped out more of each other than the Klan ever wiped out. The numbers are very clear on that. That's why the urgency exists for us to start talking about the issue of Black on Black crime. And this is one of those problems we cannot blame it on "da' Whiteman."

Despite our proclivity, this is where we have to turn inward. We have a problem with Black folks killing other Black folks and this is not something that we can blame on "the system" or blame on the White man. It is one of those unique problems that exist amongst Black communities that we have to do something about. Finally, the real problem on this issue, as we all know, is that Black folks witness these crimes and when the cops come around, nobody wants to say anything.

People witnessed Tupac being murdered and

nobody said anything in Las Vegas. Hundreds of folks were standing on the corner of Wilshire and Fairfax in L.A. when Biggie got popped. Folks were standing around looking, and the cops were investigating. They had a press conference last night to state that nobody is cooperating. Nobody is saying anything. I certainly understand that fear element. No one wants to put himself in the middle of something.

On the other hand, across the country, not just in cases involving Black celebrities, when people witness things that happen and nobody says anything, it only exacerbates the problem. If people know they can walk in the neighborhood and come on the street corner and pop somebody in broad daylight and nobody will say anything, then that kind of behavior will continue until somebody stands up and tells what they saw. Everybody knows exactly what house Dante lives in, they know who was driving the car, but nobody comes forth and says anything. And that is what puts us between a rock and a hard place.

The only thing that's going to stop this Black-on-Black crime is for those of us who know things to share what we know. Otherwise, it is going to continue. Again, particularly if they know that they can do it, and know that nobody's going to say anything. That's the real issue in this whole Tupac Shakur/Biggie Smalls murder scenario.

March 20, 1997

TJMS Topic: Free Geronimo Pratt!

You know, Tom, I get a lot of mail from all over America every day, not just here at the *Tom Joyner Morning Show*, but, of course, over at *BET*. Rarely does a day go by when I don't receive mail from a Black prison inmate who swears up and down that he was wrongfully convicted of a crime. Of course, even though my heart goes out to these brothers every single day, I can never know whether or not they are all being honest. However, what I do know is that while we can always and forever ensure that we will not *commit* a crime, none of us can guarantee at any place in our lifetime, certainly as Black folks, that we won't be *accused* and convicted of a crime. One ought not to confuse one with the other.

As you all know, Geronimo Pratt, a former Black Panther Party leader, was convicted twenty-four years ago of shooting a school teacher to death in a 1968 robbery in Santa Monica. Pratt was represented back in 1972 by a young attorney named Johnnie L. Cochran.

This is the case Cochran said he never gave up on. As a matter of fact, if you read Johnnie Cochran's book, *Journey to Justice*, he spends the entire introduction of his book talking not about the case that he won, but the case that he lost back in 1972. He swore to Geronimo Pratt, through some prison bars, that he would never forget about him. And now we see that after six habeas petitions being denied down through the years, Geronimo Pratt was finally given a hearing which lasted about four weeks and during which we learned something quite interesting.

It turns out that a Black man named Julius C.

"Julio" Butler, a guy who was the prosecution's key witness, testified at the original trial that he had never been an informant for law enforcement. But FBI documents released years after Pratt's trial showed Butler, a former Los Angeles County Sheriff's Deputy and a rival of Pratt's in the Panther Party, had been giving information to agents for more than two years prior to Geronimo Pratt's conviction.

Indeed three jurors, who were sitting in the case in 1972 said that they would never have convicted Geronimo Pratt had they known that Julio Butler, a Black man, had contact with and provided information to FBI agents. We also know now, through a little bit of research, that there are two precedent-setting cases and appellate decisions, one called *Duran* and one called *Steinberg*, where "prosecutorial misconduct" resulted in convictions being overturned. So, there are a couple of cases on the books that can be used as precedents in this case.

Johnnie L. Cochran and his defense team flew back to L.A. last week and posed the final argument in this case to give Geronimo Pratt a new hearing. Apparently the judge is set to make a decision, perhaps, even before Easter. How many of us know people whom we believe have been framed and set up for crimes they, in fact, did not commit?

There is not a whole lot you can do this morning. I am not doing this commentary to ask you to send a letter or to call somebody. The hearing is over. we are now waiting for a judge's decision. I don't mean to preach this morning, but this is clearly one of the cases where all we can really do as a Black community is sit back and pray that justice will finally be served for Geronimo Pratt, and all those brothers who were wrongfully accused and convicted.

Geronimo Pratt's case is an example, one that we can point to perhaps years down the road, to help obtain the release of other brothers who are sitting behind bars for crimes they did not commit. So, as I said, all we can really do is pray, cross our fingers, or whatever else you believe in, that Geronimo Pratt will finally be given a new trial at the least. All he's asking for is a new trial to prove that he was in fact set up by this FBI informant.

I just want us to send all of our best wishes and prayers out that Geronimo Pratt will finally get a trial so the evidence that was hidden twenty-seven years ago will finally come to light. Johnnie L. Cochran is still on the case. Perhaps, that's why he called his book, *Journey to Justice.*

Afterthought: *Geronimo Pratt JiJaga was later released after twenty-seven years in prison, and honored me by making an appearance on my* BET *program—his first live television interview with viewer phone calls. The next morning he joined us live on the* Tom Joyner Morning Show. *Pratt JiJaga surprised me by telling me that we shared the same birthday, September 13. I make it a point now to always call him and wish him a happy one.*

March 25, 1997

TJMS Topic: Cuba, The Academy and the Movie Industry

All jokes aside, let me start by congratulating Cuba Gooding, Jr. on his much deserved Academy Award last night. Now that he has won the film industry's most coveted prize, we will see if Hollywood will indeed "show Cuba the money." I have laughed more than a few times as many of my White friends over the last couple of months have acted as if *they* had discovered Cuba Gooding, Jr. in *Jerry McGuire*. If I had a dime for every time one of my White friends said to me, "Tavis, you've got to go see this guy Cuba Gooding, Jr. in *Jerry McGuire*..."

The film, *Jerry McGuire*, has made this guy a household name. Indeed, the new issue of Vanity Fair profiles Cuba Gooding, Jr. as "the next big thing." Now having said all that, I've got to tell you that outside of Cuba, or at least seeing what was going to happen to Cuba, the only thing that kept me up last night was knowing that I had a live show to do on *BET* at 11:00 p.m. Eastern. We all know too well how Hollywood treats, or for that matter, mistreats, the Black creative community. And how very few positive images of us there are reflected on the big screen. The lack of balance in the portrayal of Black America is at this point an old story.

Unfortunately, it seems to me that we always discuss our Hollywood misfortune as if we are helpless and hopeless to really do anything about it. Even though the statistics show that Black folks make up 12% of the U.S. population, but make up 25%, a full one-quarter, of the box office. One thing is certain, as my Big Momma always says, "If we keep doing what we've always done, we'll keep getting what we've always got."

So what should we do? I just want to remind us of a few simple suggestions that we already know, but we really need to practice in earnest if we are serious about making Hollywood do right by Black America. One, we need to stop seeing some of the mess that Hollywood puts out which depicts us as less than who or what we are, including the movies written, produced and directed by Black folks. Hello!

Two, check your ticket when you buy it. If you pay for one thing, but your ticket says something else, make sure they change it to the right one.

Three, don't buy these pirated or bootleg movies.

Four, make sure you go, whenever you can, to opening weekend. We've heard this a thousand times, but it is important that you get out over opening weekend. Make the effort to get there whenever you can as soon as the movie opens.

Five, write a letter. You know one thing I know now from doing television is that one letter, in most movie and television industry circles, represents or can represent as many as one thousand viewers. You've got to write letters. Check out who the studio is that produced the movie during the credits and make sure you write a letter if you enjoyed the movie, and if you didn't enjoy it for that matter. Let the studios know how you felt about it.

Six, make sure you see a variety of Black films. I know sometimes that's a lot easier said than done, but make sure you see a great variety of Black films so that Black folks who are acting in different genres can know that Black America appreciates their efforts.

And finally, here's something I think we already do anyway, and that is to tell your family and friends if you like the movie. Make sure the word of mouth spreads in the community and that other Black folks go, see and reward those Black actors on the screen who are trying to put their best foot forward.

By using these suggestions maybe next year at Oscar time we will have more to celebrate than what we had this year.

> **Afterthought:** *WRONG! It only got worse in 1998. Samuel L. Jackson and Debbie Morgan of* Eve's Bayou *and Djimon Hounsou of* Amistad *were all overlooked as actors, as were the films in which they starred.*

February 17, 1998

TJMS Topic: Do the White Thing!

Many times before, you have heard me refer on this program to racism as the most intractable, the most egregious, and the most divisive issue in America. With all due respect to W.E.B. DuBois during Black History Month, the problem of the 21st Century will also be a problem of the color line. Why? Because although racism is a learned behavior and can be prevented, for some reason we keep teaching it. For some, it is a requirement, and for others, it is an elective. But the sooner we take it off the American studies curriculum the better off we'll be.

Now having said that, I also believe there are times when we get a little footloose and careless throwing the "R" word at random. We would do well to remember that the "R" word can make like a boomerang and come back to bite you in the behind. We might also want to remember what happened to the boy who cried wolf one too many times, and be a bit more judicious in our use of the "R" word.

I offer these remarks as a preface so you would all know that I gave some time and some thought to my use of the "R" word this morning. How can I put this? Well, once again, it's Oscar time, and once again the Academy can be counted on to do the "White thing." Is the Academy racist? I don't know, you tell me. We Black folks who make up 12% of the American population, and as much as 25% of the movie-going public, constitute less than 4% of all Academy members. The folks, of course, who nominate and choose the Oscar winners. I guess they figure if we ain't in it, we can't win it. We make up less than 3% of the Directors Guild and Writers Guild members. We make up less than 2% of Local 44, one of the entertainment industry's biggest craft unions. In its seventy-year history, only six Black folks have ever won an Oscar. Not one for best actress, only one for best actor, only one ever nominated for best director, and he didn't win. Of course, Spike Lee is this year nominated for his wonderful documentary, *Four Little Girls*, which you have to go out and see. But seventy years of history here. I think the Klan may have more Black members than the Academy.

Will somebody tell me what Samuel L. Jackson has to do to get nominated for an Oscar? We all know they played Jackson in 1994 opposite John Travolta in *Pulp Fiction*. Gave him a nomination for best supporting actor, when he was on screen more than John Travolta. And I love John Travolta, but how you going to play Samuel L. Jackson? What about *Eve's Bayou*? The top-grossing American independent film of 1997, Black or White. Debbie Morgan, Angie from *All My Children*, is brilliant in that movie. What about Pam Greer in *Jackie Brown*? What about Djimon Honnsou in *Amistad*? What about Steven Spielberg for *Amistad*? I don't understand this. Does Spielberg suddenly become a horrible director when he works with a Black cast? Anything else he does turns to gold, the boy's got the Midas touch. But let him touch something Black like *Color Purple* or *Amistad* and everybody forgets the talent of Steven Spielberg.

I don't know what the answer to this problem is. I can only tell you what I'm doing. I don't care what the movie is nominated for, if I haven't seen it by now, I'm not going to see it. I can't tell you what to do, but I'm not rushing out, as I do each year to see every movie the Academy wants you to see in time for Oscar night. Not this year. It's time for the Academy to stop playing all these brilliant Black actors.

April 1, 1997

TJMS Topic: Jackie Roosevelt Robinson: Athlete, Activist and Role Model

Today is April Fool's Day, but this is no joke. Today is also opening day at Dodger's Stadium in Chavez Ravine out in Los Angeles. And whether you are a Dodger fan or not, this is a day of special celebration, because what we are celebrating is so much bigger than baseball itself, especially if you're African American. Believe it or not, it was fifty years ago with the start of the season today that Jackie Roosevelt Robinson became the first Black man to play major league baseball. In 1947, he took the field for the Brooklyn Dodgers against the Boston Braves.

Robinson had actually been signed two years earlier by the Dodgers, even though at the time fifteen of the sixteen teams voted against integrating the

"White man's game." Robinson was picked personally by Branch Rickey, the Dodger's general manager, who was looking for a special player, as he said, "to integrate the game." He wanted the player who had the courage not to respond during his first two seasons to the many acts of virulent racism and open hostility which was certain to come in his face. To be sure, Robinson was threatened physically, as well as taunted, insulted and demeaned. Say nothing of his having to lodge and eat in the Negro section of town everywhere he went because most hotels and restaurants refused to serve him in 1947.

And yet against all the odds, number forty-two went on to be voted Rookie of the Year, National League Most Valuable Player (MVP) in 1949, and to be entered into the Baseball Hall of Fame in the very first year of his eligibility after playing ten seasons of major league ball. Time doesn't permit me to give Jackie Robinson all the props that he deserves this morning. But I think a few things very quickly are worth noting. One, while Jackie Robinson was the player chosen to integrate major league baseball, he wasn't the only Negro League player who had the talent to play the White man's game. What Jackie Robinson was given was not just talent from God, but he was also given the opportunity to prove his worth.

And even today, we need to recognize that talent without opportunity is like a car without gas. If people give us the opportunity, I know that most of us can deliver on every single chance. But be clear about one fact, when Jackie Robinson did get the opportunity, he delivered. Whether we like it or not, because so few of us even in 1997, fifty years later, really get an opportunity in certain walks of life, we need to recognize that our performance can either close the door in the face of another African American, or open the door just a little bit wider.

So many of today's athletes and entertainers are afraid to take a stand on matters of social and political consequence. Jackie Robinson was not one of those persons. He was very involved in the Civil Rights Movement and, in fact, was a dear friend of Dr. King. He was not afraid to take a stand.

Although much has changed in fifty years, much has not. In many ways baseball is still a White man's game at least off the field. Only 20% of the game's non-playing personnel are people of color. There are four managers of color on the field and only one general manager (GM). It's sad but it's true. And speaking of GMs, the only Black general manager in major league baseball is a guy named Bob Watson of the New York Yankees—the defending World Champion New York Yankees, I might add. Who said we aren't qualified and that we can't deliver?

I think Robinson's courage under fire, especially those first two years, proved once again that to whom much is given much is required. And every Black child in America who aspires to be an athlete this morning ought to be told about Jackie Robinson. In fact, his autobiography, *I Never Had It Made,* is going to be re-released this month in paperback. Now if Mark Fuhrman's book can sit atop *The New York Times* bestseller list, I better pull up. Can I get a witness? If Mark Fuhrman's book can sit atop *The New York Times* bestseller list, then Jackie Robinson's book, *I Never Had It Made,* ought to be bought by every Black person in America and shared with every Black kid who aspires to be an athlete. We have to do a better job in our community of letting folks know who Jackie Roosevelt Robinson was and what he did. Not just for Black America but what he did for America as a whole. Thank God for Jackie Robinson.

Afterthought: *Sometimes I struggle to deliver on air*

the passion I feel deep inside. This was one of those days. I just think we, and certainly professional athletes, owe Jackie Robinson a debt we can never repay. But too many Black athletes aren't even trying.

May 13, 1997

TJMS Topic: Reflections On My Trip to South Africa

This morning, I'd like to offer, if I can, a brief postscript on our trip to South Africa last week. Tom, as you recall, we had some pretty heated and in-depth discussions, most definitely off the air, about the Truth and Reconciliation Commission (TRC). The TRC is offering amnesty to those who confess to political crimes committed during the apartheid era. Last Saturday as we were departing that country, South Africa's deadline to seek immunity arrived. Some 8,000 South Africans actually met the deadline with approximately 2,000 applications coming at the 11th hour, so to speak. Almost a third came in at the last minute.

It makes you wonder how many folks are really apologetic about the crimes that they committed against humanity during the period of White minority rule. Not to mention that only a handful of senior members of the apartheid era governments applied for amnesty. Even the African National Congress, (ANC) Mandela's party, admitted to 550 acts of violence in its fight to end apartheid. What an irony, the victims confess and the perpetrators take the proverbial fifth.

But enough on the TRC, you don't want me to get started on that this morning. I still think that at the very least some form of community service is in order. Some form of recompense for those who tortured, raped, bombed and otherwise abused the good people of South Africa.

A quick final thought. We now know—despite what we read in our newspapers, see on our televisions, and hear on our radios—that all the news coming out of the African continent is not bad news. We, the African American community, need to challenge and champion more balanced coverage about the African continent. Excuse my Ebonics for a moment, but it ain't all about starvation, tribal warfare, violence and dictatorship.

We certainly have to make sure that when we see those kinds of atrocities that we call those things out. Ultimately, I think we have to push for more in-depth stories and more in-depth coverage about South Africa. For example, while we were there last week, Mandela's third anniversary as president came around. There were no major stories about that. We now know from having visited Capetown that it is one of the cities bidding for the 2004 Olympics. Not a lot of coverage about that. So there are some positive stories coming out of South Africa and the African continent in general. I thank you again, Tom, for taking me last week. I had a wonderful time in South Africa. When are we going back?

June 3, 1997

TJMS Topic: Betty Shabazz

Tom, what can you say about the trail of tragedy which seems to follow Dr. Betty Shabazz? I don't even know where one begins in trying to express one's feelings about a sister who has surely tested the thesis that God does not put more on us than we can bear. Let me commence this morning as I did on the show last night by extending our best wishes and sending up our prayers for Dr. Betty Shabazz as she fights for her life in New York's Jacobi Medical Center.

I know how sensitive this issue is at the moment for all of us in Black America, but I believe that there are lessons in every dilemma that can help us turn our pain into power if we are willing to do so. Consequently, my thoughts this morning are simply these:

I think that the twelve-year-old namesake of Malcolm X is as his attorney, Percy Sutton, has said, "A child covering up his head, wishing it hadn't happened, wanting to make it all go away." Malcolm Shabazz is clearly a disturbed and troubled young Black boy, not unlike countless others who are not the grandsons of Malcolm X, but who nonetheless need our love, attention, support and, most importantly, parental guidance.

I think Malcolm's mother, Qubilah Shabazz, has her own issues. Once charged with plotting to kill Minister Louis Farrakhan, Qubilah has undergone psychological and substance abuse counseling.

I think Qubilah has every reason to be psychologically disturbed after witnessing the assassination of her father.

I think the Black community, in general, does not deal well with emotional and mental duress. And for too many of us, substance abuse is the only therapy that we know.

I think Qubilah is still hurting and needs to heal. I think a lot of Black folks are just like Qubilah, whether they acknowledge it or not.

I think the matter of how we raise and discipline our children in the 90s and beyond really is not an issue, but it ought to be.

I think our pain over the loss of great Black leaders like Malcolm, Martin and Medger pales in comparison to the pain felt by Betty, Coretta and Myrlie. They had to deal with grieving in public. They had to deal with the folks who hated their husbands in life and death. They had to deal with raising children by themselves. They had to deal with providing for their family without significant financial inheritance. And then, they had to deal with seeking vindication and searching for the truth about the tragedies which took away their spouses. It was Betty Shabazz, as you recall, who went in search of the truth about the plot to kill Malcolm. It was Coretta Scott King in court just a few weeks ago trying to find out what James Earl Ray really knew. And it was Myrlie Evers who fought to bring De La Beckwith back to trial yet again, and eventually to justice.

I think this tragedy which now engulfs the family of Malcolm X in some form engulfs a lot of Black families. I think Betty Shabazz is a strong proud Black woman. I think Betty Shabazz is a fighter. I think we all need to pray for the family of Malcolm X and for Black families everywhere.

September 4, 1997

TJMS Topic: Reflections on Diana's Tragic Death

The untimely death of Diana, the Princess of Wales, was tragic. This horrible tragedy has the world talking about a variety of subjects, and I have a couple of words to say about it, if I may. It is my sense, and I admittedly can be totally wrong about this, that this tragedy has not been the kind of passionate office water cooler conversation with some Americans as it has been with others. Perhaps, this is because some of us don't know exactly where we fit into the conversation or just how we relate to the specific subjects which are involved in this tragedy.

Comparatively speaking, we've been rather quiet around here on the *Tom Joyner Morning Show* about this terrible incident. But not at all because any of us are unsympathetic to the unfortunate situation. Clearly none of us has ever been insulated from the pain of loss, we all know that. As Black folks, we have all been gripped by grief at some point no matter how peripheral. There is something about this particular tragedy, however that leaves many of us to feeling peripheral to this particular issue.

I happened to be in Atlanta backstage at the Civic Center with J., George, Myra, Miss Dupree and Sybil from the *Tom Joyner Morning Show* when this story broke. I can tell you whoever was not on stage at that time was squeezed next to Sybil and me backstage watching the television as this story unfolded. Now I don't speak for my colleagues, certainly this group of characters, but I think we were all backstage glued to this television screen, clearly and visibly shaken. We were shocked. I ended up excusing myself, leaving the concert early to go back to the hotel to really watch this, because I figured on *CNN* the next day we were going to change topics and talk about this, which in fact, we did. We were all equally stunned by this story, so it's not that we don't feel the loss. But for some reason, we're not, I think, connected to this particular story.

Having said that, there are three or four things about the story, beyond the actual accident, that I do want to comment on. One, this whole propensity to beat up on the tabloids. Very simply, somebody is publishing this nonsense and somebody is purchasing this nonsense, and it seems to me it would be an easy task to beat up on the tabloids, the paparazzi and the stalkarazzi. That's the easy part. The difficult part is trying to challenge all of us, all Americans, to be more conscious about what we buy. That's Black citizens, White citizens, and everybody else. Two, with respect to this whole conversation now that we see brewing about privacy laws, or as the Brits would say, "preevacy" laws. I am the wrong person to be talking to about retreating in any way on First Amendment rights to free speech. I don't know how you balance this out, giving people their freedom yet not allowing people to be harassed. Certainly celebrities have the right to not be harassed, such as when the private confines of their own home are invaded with a super long photo lens. I think that's unconscionable and untenable.

The point is, if you start retreating on the First Amendment, giving certain people certain privacy laws, it becomes a very, very slippery slope, especially for Black folks. I'm not about to give up any rights with regard to the First Amendment. And, I'm bothered by the fact that the media in this case is not doing enough to condemn drinking and driving.

That burns me up. I mean, the tragedy aside —that's bad enough—but these networks and everybody else are still spending more time talking about the tragedy than the lessons that I think ought to be learned from the tragedy. We ought to be doing 24/7 commercials and commentaries and analyses about the dangers of drinking and driving and not enough of us have gone there as far as I'm concerned.

And finally, with all due respect to celebrities and my celebrity friends like J., George, Sybil and so forth, you cannot complain about the press impeding and intruding on your right to privacy, then use the press everytime you want to get your message out, or spin your issue. You can't have it both ways. This is a horrible and ugly situation. I think we all feel the pain of Diana's loss, but for some reason there are some Americans who are gripped more by this whole scenario. Others, for some reason, still feel somewhat peripheral to this incident. I hope I've made some sense to you. I've been struggling with this.

Afterthought: *Diana's death wasn't necessarily an incident or issue at the top of the African American agenda, but I thought there were a few interesting points worth making, so I did.*

ADVOCACY

September 26, 1996

Tom Joyner Morning Show Topic: The Next Frontier

Ostensibly, Tom, every political election is supposed to be about the future. Yet, in most political races, we see candidates spending all of their time talking about issues already on the table, things like abortion, affirmative action, the economy or even crime. Or worse yet, they spend all their time longing for the good old days which, as we all know, weren't so good for most of us in the first place.

Today though, I want to quickly highlight three issues that nobody is really talking about, but they are things I think we are going to be debating on the battleground of the future that we need to start considering right now.

First, for those of you riding on the information superhighway, you should know that here in Washington there is a debate brewing. This escalating debate is about who is going to control the data flow. What should and what should not, what will and what will not be allowed on the Internet. And while we have to keep a very close eye on abuse of the Internet and try to do everything we can against hate speech and other patently objectionable material, we cannot surrender, by our absence at the polls, control of the data flow to politicians who are hostile to our best interests. We understand very clearly in our community that information is power, and we just can't not show up at the polls and thus surrender control of the debate about who is going to control the Internet.

Second, keep an ear open for politicians on the Right attacking multiculturalism and diversity. And what I mean by multiculturalism is an equal respect for all cultures and allowing each individual to determine the significance of his or her origins on their present life and heritage. The assault that we hear increasingly about diversity in this country is going to snag Black folks. Indeed, already there are folks in Washington who are whispering about doing away with African American Studies programs on Black campuses. They want to target these programs for "re-imposing segregation in higher education."

Now we all know that's nonsense. The only reason these Black studies programs existed in the first place is because too often what we are taught on college campuses with regard to U.S. history is selective in its memory. It's unfair, it's inaccurate, and because of this, we created Black studies programs. But when you hear people talking about "deracializing higher education," what they are really talking about is doing away with Black studies programs across the country and that's a dangerous thing.

Finally, in the aftermath of the O.J. Simpson trial, we now see states increasingly trying to pass laws for non-unanimous jury verdicts. In other words, instead of having all twelve people agree to find one guilty, most states are now attempting to lower the burden of proof for guilt. We may go down to ten, we may go down to nine, or it may be majority wins. This would even be for criminal cases, and that is the worst thing, given the fact that we already know that Black folks are disproportionately targeted for sentencing.

The worst thing that can happen to Black folks in terms of criminal justice is for the burden of proof to be lowered to less than twelve. If you can't get twelve folks to agree on a verdict, then maybe it's not that the brother was guilty. Maybe it's that your evidence just doesn't hold up.

Those are three issues I wanted to highlight

that we need to keep in the back of our minds. Watch, listen and ask, when you get a chance, where politicians stand on your issues. Start to look toward the future and beyond the issues that we are talking about right now.

Afterthought: *I figure Black folks in America can always use a head start. So I try, when possible, to get ahead of the curve by keeping our audience in the know as best I can. As I write this notation, Jesse Jackson is calling for a halt to a proposed $37 billion merger of MCI and WorldCom. If the merger happens, just two companies would control a staggering 60% of the Internet backbone. WorldCom is the only major U.S. telecommunications company with no minorities or women on its fifteen member board.*

October 29, 1996

TJMS Topic: Election Day Top Ten

Election Day is one week from today, and I thought that we would put together a short list of things that everybody who is going to the polls next week can do between now and next Tuesday. None of this is rocket science; it's all very simple. But we continue to get mail and phone calls about what people can do beyond simply going to the polls.

Number one, take everybody in your house. Tom has been saying this repeatedly over the last few months. Make sure everybody in your house who is registered to vote is going to the polls. Number two, try to get at least ten other people to go to the polls. We all know ten people in our church, in our school, in our neighborhoods. Just make ten phone calls to let folks know Election Day is a week from today and to make sure they get to the polls.

Tom asked you to get five folks registered. We know you did that. But now just make ten phone calls to remind people that next Tuesday, a week from today, is Election Day.

Third, take at least five people between the ages of 18 to 24. We have to get young people involved in the process. We got many of them registered this time around, but now we need to remind them that either before they go to school, before they go to work, or after they finish their day next Tuesday, they've got to go to the polls.

Fourth, take your grandchildren, take your nieces, your nephews, take young folks who are not yet of voting age (which is 18) to the polls with you to understand the experience of what it is like to participate in the process. Start to put that in them right now.

Fifth, encourage, as Tom said earlier, your friends, your neighbors and your co-workers to go to the polls. Remind people who you are going to see between now and next Tuesday that Tuesday is Election Day.

Six, remind every single brother who went to the Million Man March, or who lied and said he went, or brothers who bragged about the Million Man March and how successful it was, to remember what that was all about and to get to the polls and vote.

Number seven, you may want to read the October issue of *Emerge* magazine. *Emerge* did a wonderful thing in the October issue which was to put together a report card on House members and Senate members who have over 20% Black folks in their districts and how they voted during the last Congress. So you may want to check out *Emerge* magazine to see how your particular representative or senator did.

Eight, if you go to one of those churches that believe that the only work of the church is inside its four walls on Sunday and raising an offering and taking your tithes, make sure that your minister reminds people this Sunday in church that Tuesday is Election Day. I go to a very activist church, but some churches aren't as activist as others. But this coming Sunday morning ask your minister to remind the parishioners that Tuesday is, in fact, Election Day.

Nine, vote by absentee ballot. I happened to vote yesterday. I finally got it done. I did my absentee ballot and sent it back in. So you can still in many states vote by absentee ballot or at least go downtown and vote early if you don't have time to go next Tuesday.

Number ten, make sure you read up and study the issues before you actually go to the polls. There's nothing worse than going in the booth and having to spend an hour in there because you've not familiarized yourself with the candidates or with the issues.

We've got to get beyond playing what we call plantation politics, waiting till the day before the election to get one of those slate mailers in your mailbox and just voting the way Congressman so-and-so said, or Senator so-and-so said, or Councilwoman so-and-so said. Learn the issues, familiarize yourself with the ballot measures, with the candidates. So when you go to the polls next Tuesday, it won't take you a half an hour, and you can get in and out within five minutes.

Afterthought: *A lot of folk requested copies of this particular commentary which surprised me a bit. Then again, practical and common sense advice isn't all that common these days in politics.*

November 7, 1996

TJMS Topic: Election Postmortem

Today I want to give my final postscript on Tuesday's elections. We now know that despite all the efforts we made here, and we made some great ones, just under half of all eligible voters across the country, that is everybody, not just Black folks, turned out to the polls on Tuesday. That is the lowest turnout since the early 1920s. The turnout was down in every state, and as you might suspect, turnout in the African American community, unfortunately, was even worse.

While we had a few shining moments on Tuesday, we lost big, as we said yesterday, in California on the affirmative action initiative. As we've known affirmative action over the last twenty-five years, we will know it no more. It is now a thing of the past in California. And I think that we can expect the attack on affirmative action to be coming to a state near you sometime soon.

I'm almost to the point now that I'm ashamed to tell folks I vote in California given what happened on Tuesday. And it wasn't even a close race. It was a whipping; We lost that battle on affirmative action in California by about 64% on Tuesday.

Also, in the 104th Congress, there were thirty-eight Black members. In the new 105th Congress, there will only be thirty-six Black members. And, Newt Gingrich is still in control of the House.

As I thought about the fact that these were the last presidential elections of this century and that we had again lost these important elections by the margin of our absence at the polls, it made me wonder. I thought in my own crazy way, what would it actually take to get Black folks to the polls in record numbers?

Five things came to mind, and these are just rhetorical questions. What if they wanted to dishonor Dr. King by repealing the Martin Luther King, Jr. holiday? Would we go to the polls then? What if they said again that only property owners could vote?

No matter what your stake in the electoral process is, if you don't own property, you can't vote. Would that get us out? What if they wanted to re-institute slavery? I'm almost to the point where I wonder whether or not we would turn out at a decent rate if they put forth a pro-slavery bill.

What if they wanted to, once again, make segregation—separate-but-equal—the law of the land? Would that get us to the polls? And what if, as we mentioned the other day, they made us vote and if you didn't vote, you'd be fined or face jail time, as they do in certain countries? Would we get to the polls then, or would the prisons be even more overcrowded with Black folks?

Now a lot of folks listening would say Tavis has lost his mind. These things could never happen, would never happen in this country. Well, I would argue that when you start down the slippery slope of letting things like affirmative action go, battles that we thought we had won twenty-five to thirty years ago, begin again, I submit to you that anything and everything in this country is possible.

I will leave you with the words of the late Dr. Benjamin Elijah Mays, President of Morehouse College, who once said, "He who starts behind in the great race of life must forever remain behind or run faster than the man in front." It's time for us to pick up the pace.

November 12, 1996

TJMS Topic: Texaco

It's cold outside this morning in Washington, but I'm hot on the inside. We have all been following this developing story regarding the Texaco executives who originally were accused of using racial slurs to demean African Americans. The story on all the front pages today is that we are now told by Texaco officials that the "n" word was not in fact used, and what was actually said was "St. Nicholas." I'm trying to figure that out, how the "n" word sounds like St. Nicholas. Furthermore, I don't know that playing Santa Claus this close to Christmas is the right thing to do, but that's what we were told yesterday by these Texaco officials.

A few observations, if I can. First of all, if Texaco were as quick to place African Americans in key executive positions as they were to deny that the "n" word was ever used, this might just be a bad dream to begin with. Second, this case really isn't about who did or did not use the "n" word. Indeed, both sides in this case have experts who differ on what was said. Surprise, surprise.

It's about widespread discrimination at Texaco. It's about executives who are on tape laughing at the concept of diversity and talking about destroying documents regarding Black employment. It's about the number of Black-owned Texaco franchises. It is, once again, about this thing called the glass ceiling that we know far too well.

Additionally, last evening, a Texaco executive was scheduled to be on *BET* to talk for the first time to Black America directly about this case. At the eleventh hour, Texaco called to pull out on doing the show. They cancel their appearance to talk to Black America. I guess they didn't learn from Bob Dole snubbing the NAACP. I think it was grossly insensitive, but at the eleventh hour last night they called and said, "We're not going to do the show." And that was that.

Finally, for those who were suggesting last week that affirmative action is no longer necessary, that affirmative action is a thing of the past and has outlived its usefulness and doesn't matter anymore, here we are now, just a week later, talking about no executives of African American descent in top positions at Texaco.

This is what happens when you don't have folks in the room to check that kind of behavior when folks start sitting around talking about Black folks. That's why affirmative action is so necessary, and that's why last Tuesday I was so upset that we lost Prop. 209 in California. I should add another thing. I'm tempted to say that the explosion yesterday at a Texaco refinery in California means that God don't like ugly.

For those who want to respond to Texaco directly, and I hope this is an issue where Black folks can be activists and take a role in letting this company know how we feel about this incident, I have an address and a phone number which I will give to you. The phone number to call Texaco at their corporate headquarters is (914) 253-6170. That's (914) 253-6170. I encourage you to call. And for those who want to write a letter, because these folks do respond to their mail as well as their phone calls, the address is: Texaco, Inc., 2000 Westchester Avenue, White Plains, NY 10650.

Afterthought: *What I love most on the* Tom Joyner Morning Show *is reminding Black folks that politics is not a spectator sport. As Big Momma says,*

"You can't win it if you ain't in it!" Get involved! Now! By the way, Peter Bijur, the Chairman and CEO of Texaco, Inc., must have grown weary of hearing from our listeners. Following this commentary, he appeared on BET...twice!

June 12, 1997

TJMS Topic: Black, Proud and Rescuing Positive Black Images

Let me begin, Tom, by asking everyone listening this morning if you are Black and proud? Only if you are Black and proud, get a piece of paper and a pencil handy right quick. In just a moment, I want to share some information with you so you don't want to be scrambling two minutes from now to grab some paper and a pen to write it down. So if you are Black and proud, get ready to scribble down some information in just a second here.

Too often Black folks are caught in a position of being reactive, as we all know. It sometimes disturbs me when I offer commentary here that we just simply get put in a position of being reactive. In fact, sometimes we put ourselves in those awkward positions, but this morning, for a change, we have a unique opportunity to be proactive. My grandmother, Big Momma, always likes to tell me that right is right and don't wrong nobody. Well, once again, Black folks are about to be wronged. But we have a chance right now, a brief window, to right the situation, if we have the will. That is, the will to write.

You may not be aware that the number one and number two shows for Black Americans on television may not return to the airways next fall. That's right, both *Living Single* and *New York Undercover* have been scheduled as mid-season replacements on the *Fox* network which basically means that they will only reappear if something else doesn't work. Why, you might ask, would the *Fox* network pull the number one and number two shows in Black America? Well let me give you the short answer. It's cheaper to replace these shows than to renew these shows (rising talent costs), and they know that Black folks, quite frankly, will watch whatever Black replacements they air.

You see the *Fox* network has gotten shrewd these days because they recognize that if they don't replace these Black shows with something else Black, we are going to yell racism. So they will replace them with Black shows to stop that from happening. Kind of slick, huh? Yeah, about as slick as sandpaper. Because we know that this is more about economics than racism. This is about money, honey.

They will continue to pay the stars, of say, *90210* but dis the brothers and sisters on *New York Undercover* and *Living Single.* Make no mistake about this, this is an absolute affront to Black America. These shows represent positive images for Black people. Something we certainly don't see enough of on television or in the movies. They represent positive images. Khadijah owns her own magazine on *Living Single*, Malik Yoba on *New York Undercover* spends time with his son. I can go on and on and on, but I'm preaching to the choir here. Y'all watch these shows; you know the positive images they represent. And yet we see these shows under attack, being removed from the schedule. The number one and number two shows in Black America sitting somewhere collecting dust only scheduled to return if something else doesn't work.

Here's what we need to do. Get your pen or your pencil right quick. We did this on Texaco. We did it with the voter registration drive. Here is a chance for us to do it again and to be proactive. And if I know our listeners, I know the people are going to do what we are asking them to do. Write a letter. It can be a short letter. I sent one yesterday on-line (www.fox.com). Address your letter to: Peter Roth, President, Fox Entertainment Group, 10201 West Pico Boulevard, Los Angeles, CA 90035.

Write Mr. Roth even a one sentence letter, saying "Mr. Roth please bring back *Living Single* and *New York Undercover*, my favorite two shows, on air." As you well know, Tom, all they really care about is the volume. Mr. Roth isn't going to read all these letters, but he certainly has to receive them. They have to know that Black folks are upset about being dissed once again by the networks. There is no reason this ought to happen. It ain't right. You know it ain't right, I know it ain't right. And the only way it's going to be corrected is if we sit down and write some letters. Don't try to call. Write letters! It can be one sentence, but get that letter out. I swear to you, I am not going to let this thing die for the next few weeks until Mr. Roth is sitting in mail! We cannot allow the networks to continue to disrespect us, particularly around shows that portray positive images of Black people. It's not right, but it will continue to happen if we don't do something about it. Not to mention that I want to see Uncle Tibby back next fall.

Afterthought: *This commentary started a national campaign to bringing back two popular Black television programs. By now, most know about the success we later had in bringing back Living Single, thanks to Newsweek, U.S. News & World Report, Ebony and Jet, but it took a while. Read on and take note of the dates on the next two entries.*

July 10, 1997

TJMS Topic: Top Five *Fox* Questions

I just want to do a quick update, Tom. Don't you hate it when people don't follow through, when they don't give you an update? I thought I'd hit this *Fox* thing again. Because so many have been asking me questions, and I know that they've been asking you questions about the campaign too. I've kind of whittled this down to the five questions, the five *Fox network* questions that I get asked most often. So let me try to answer them as best I can.

How is the campaign going? It's going great! We continue to get word from *Fox* network, from our operatives in the *Fox* network mailroom. The brothers, you know, who are receiving your letters everyday. The mailroom is always run by brothers, man, I don't care where it is. Except at *BET*, there are White guys running the mailroom! Equal employment opportunity, you know. Anyway we continue to get word from *Fox* that the letters are pouring in every single day, so in terms of your participation in getting those letters written and mailed, we appreciate it. The letter writing campaign in that regard is going very well.

I get asked all the time what's up with Peter Roth? Is he going to come on Tom's program to try to explain this nonsense to the African American community, as to why the number one and number two shows in Black viewing households are being put on the shelf? The answer is, I don't know. As a matter of fact, I'm going to follow up with Mr. Roth's office today and find out why they have not responded. Also, I'm going to find out whether or not he is, in fact, going to take a minute of his time to come and explain to our audience the unexplainable.

What are the chances of our being successful with the campaign? That's a good question. First of all, I don't know the answer to that question, but I can tell you this, if we keep doing what we've always done, we'll keep getting what we've always got. That is to say, I'm not a pessimist. I'm an optimist. And I don't think in terms of "not." But ultimately, even if we don't succeed in this campaign—though I don't think in those terms—we as a people have to get in the habit of letting folks hear from us when they think that they can get away with dissing us. As long as we're Black, there are always going to be issues around which we need to organize, strategize and mobilize, and we've got to get in the habit of flexing our muscles a little bit when it's necessary. So the letter writing campaign is always going to come in handy from time to time, issue to issue. We've got to get in that habit.

Should I keep writing letters? Is Tom the "Fly Jock"? Is Melvin in the closet? Is J. a player? Of course. Keep writing those letters! There are never enough letters going to *Fox* network. If you've written one, write them again. As a matter of fact, the next time you write, make it a little different. In your letter ask Mr. Roth, specifically, why he won't come on, or will he come on, or when is he going to come on Tom's show to explain this issue.

Finally, the last question: What's next? Well, this week, confident that each one of you has already sent in your letter, we expand the reach of our campaign by asking you to make a concerted effort this week to contact your pastor, your fraternity, your sorority, your union leader, or your youth group. Any organization or institution you belong to that has a newsletter read by Black folks. Contact these organizations and have them put this information in the newsletter. As we say all the time, the party ain't over. We don't want to go Martin on them, and so here is the address one more time: Peter Roth, President, *Fox* Entertainment Group, 10201 West Pico Boulevard, LA 90035. You have now been updated.

You've got your marching orders. Let's get those letters moving again.

> **Afterthought:** *Persistence. Big Momma always says to me, "Once a task you've first begun, never finish until it's done. Be the labor great or small, do it well or not at all."*

August 26, 1997

TJMS Topic: *Fox* Gives No Props

Let me deal with this right quick, because you know my blood is boiling already.

You have to understand why *Fox* network-would not give the credit to a whole bunch of Black folks across the country in the first place. As you can imagine, we got a number of press calls yesterday. One of the reasons why I'm in New York is to respond to press inquiries about our campaign. I've been telling people that I'm not at all surprised, particularly after having sat in the meeting with Mr. Roth. The reason is simple. When you do that, as you well know, what you really are doing is inviting Black folk to continue to write you letters when they don't like what you do. Now that takes money, it takes manpower, it takes creativity, and it takes a lot of effort to respond to all of that mail, particularly when it's negative mail.

I don't think that Mr. Roth wants to have his people expend their energy and their time responding to a bunch of Black folks's mail in the first place. Two, you will recall that they did not want to give us the credit for the campaign in the first place. As I mentioned yesterday, when this campaign started it was nonexistent as far as they were concerned. It occurred to me when I was in the meeting with him that we had gone from being nonexistent to being invited to a meeting with the President of the *Fox* network.

Now you tell me how we had nothing to do with this decision when Tavis Smiley and Tom Joyner got the phone call to come to the meeting. They didn't call anybody else to a private meeting. They called us, but we had nothing to do with the show staying on the air. They called us to a meeting and as you recall, The *Fox* television network gave us the exclusive on breaking the story yesterday. They held up their press release until we could announce it first on the *Tom Joyner Morning Show*.

Now tell me why a bunch of Black folks were given an exclusive to break the story and were invited to a private one-on-one meeting, but didn't have anything to do with this outcome. And if we did, it amounted to only 8,000 letters. They would have taken those letters and burned them if there were only 8,000 of them. It was a whole lot more than 8,000 letters. I've been asked a thousand times, how many letters did you all send? Do you have any knowledge or any idea of how many letters you sent? I answered that question the same way I answered the question as to how many Black men were at the Million Man March. In one word, ENOUGH. It was enough to get the issue of the Million Man March covered by everybody in the world. It was enough to get the television show, *Living Single*, back on the air.

And finally, let me just say this, we have to feel good about what we did. I mean you can't expect Peter Roth, or anybody else at *Fox* network to come out and say we did it because the Black folks pressured us, or we did it because the Black folks made us do it. You know how many letters you sent. You know what you did. You know how many times you e- mailed *Fox* network. You know how many times you faxed *Fox* network, and we know what you did. I've got a couple thousand carbon copies myself. People would copy me every time they sent something to *Fox* network.

I know they got more than 8,000 pieces of mail. But it's really nothing to get upset about. The bottom line is it's back on the air. We know what we did and does it really matter, quite frankly, who gets the credit? I'm not trying to take credit. Tom Joyner is not taking the credit. The credit belongs to the folks who wrote the letters. You.

So, forget what Peter Roth and *Fox* have to say. As a matter of fact, that's the very reason why when I cut the deal with him, I arranged for Mr. Roth to come on our show. I can tell you right now what the first question is going to be—how are you going to dis us and tell us we didn't have anything to do with the renewal? That's the first question. You all can get in line behind me, but I'm asking that one first. Now I've got to go calm down some.

Afterthought: *Well, we got* Living Single *back on air! But still, I was hot this morning. The folks in the Fox publicity unit refused to credit our campaign as a factor in the network's decision to bring back* Living Single. *Not to worry. Peter Roth did come on the* Tom Joyner Morning Show *and I never got to ask my question because he immediately told our audience that you the audience, did it.*

November 4, 1997

TJMS Topic: Texaco: One Year Later!

Tom, would you believe that it was exactly one year ago today that secret tapes came to light exposing executives at Texaco dissing Black folks and other employees of color and planning to destroy documents demanded in a discrimination lawsuit. One year later some folks see progress at Texaco, namely the executives and consultants at Texaco, but others aren't so sure. Since I'm not on Texaco's payroll in White Plains, New York, I'm not the one to make the case for Texaco this morning. However, I do think it's interesting to note and worthwhile in retrospect to consider two very important ironies.

First, as I look back on this rather bizarre case, I'm still fascinated by the variety of responses from Black leaders to the race discrimination lawsuit against Texaco, which to my mind, underscores the need for a collective voice and a broader perspective in organizing our political power. I've said before that Black folks don't think or speak monolithically and that's okay, but sometimes it does help to speak in unison particularly when you are trying to get paid. Consider the following: first of all, you have this brother named H. Carl McCall, the Comptroller of the state of New York. He calls Peter Bijur, Chairman and CEO of Texaco, and says he wants a copy of the independent investigation that Texaco has launched or he's going to pull out his 1.2 million shares in Texaco stock, worth $14,000,000. Then you have our friends the Reverend Jesse Jackson and the Reverend Al Sharpton who set up their own meeting with Peter Bijur at Texaco. They threatened that if there was no immediate settlement they were going to picket and boycott. Then you have our friend,

Kweisi Mfume at the NAACP, who meets separately with Peter Bijur and says he wants a report back from the company in 30 days on how they plan to improve the racial climate at Texaco.

Now, as we all know, less than two weeks after the secret recordings came out, Texaco did, in fact, agree to pay a record $140 million on the racial discrimination case. We were all fortunate in that regard. But you have to know that Mr. Bijur was confused as heck. And so with all due respect to our fine and capable Black leaders, I've said before and I'll say it again, it is scary, to think what would happen if we ever got organized as Black folks and got on the same page. I mean, in a certain respect, you've got to be laughing at the $140 million that Black folks did get. How much more could we have secured from Texaco, and I'm not just talking money; how much more could we have secured if all these Black leaders had been on the same page?

Irony number two, it is interesting to note that the lawsuit against Texaco was settled in the same month that Californians voted to end affirmative action. At first glance, these two occurrences may seem totally unrelated. Not so. The Texaco tapes in my judgment represent another example of how the attack on affirmative action and diversity is shifting from the public sector to the private sector. Make no mistake about it, when the government looks the other way, corporate America does likewise. When the government starts snoozing, corporate America starts scheming.

One year ago, it was California; one year later, it's Texas. Houston to be exact. Houston, we have a problem. Today voters in Houston go to the polls to decide whether or not they will be the first city in this country to cast aside affirmative action programs. The bottom line is that we all know somebody Black in

Houston, and I encourage you right now, during the next commercial break, to pick up the phone. If you're at work, you use the phone for everything else, use it for this purpose. Pick up the phone and call somebody in Houston right now, and tell them to wake themselves up, to get to the polls, that we are depending on them today. What happens today will cast a long shadow or a long sunbeam with regard to affirmative action as we know it. We cannot lose this election by the margin of our absence at the polls. We got slam-dunked by the Supreme Court yesterday on affirmative action, and I'm not down for getting dissed two days in a row on affirmative action.

You should know that there are twenty-six states right now that are making some progress on putting a measure similar to California's Prop. 209 on the ballot. Twenty-six other states! That's why I say what happens in Houston today will cast even a further shadow or a longer sunbeam. We cannot lose this election in Houston today. We all need to call somebody Black in Houston and say, for God's sake please make sure you go to the polls today.

Afterthought: *Black folks did go to the polls in Houston and in record numbers. The anti-affirmative action ballot measure lost miserably. On this day, Houston also set the stage to later elect its first Black mayor, Lee Brown. How good it feels!*

November 11, 1997

TJMS Topic: Christie's to Auction Slave Memorabilia

I thought, Tom, you'd like to know that tomorrow the world famous Christie's, the auction house in New York, frequented by the rich and the famous, most certainly the rich, is having an auction tomorrow morning. Nothing unusual about an auction house having an auction, but I thought you and our loyal listening audience might want to know what Christie's is actually auctioning tomorrow morning. It seems that Christie's has decided to auction off slavery memorabilia as part of the American Civil War Collection. I should say slavery paraphernalia since there ain't much memorable about slavery.

I don't exactly know where to begin because so much about Christie's decision just doesn't agree with me. Clearly, Christie's has the right in our free enterprise system to sell whatever they choose to sell. I'm always encouraging Black folks, especially those just beginning their professional careers, to aspire to Black entrepreneurship, economic independence, and so I'm not one to trash capitalism. The only thing wrong with capitalism is that they always get the capital and we always get the ism—racism, sexism, ageism—but that's another commentary for another day. Meanwhile back to Christie's. The real problem here with this decision is that these kinds of artifacts ought to be on display in an appropriate setting and used to educate folks about the horrors of slavery, not sold to the highest bidder—most likely a private collector and not a public museum.

Christie's has a house policy to not sell any paraphernalia related to the Holocaust. Now where, I ask, is the moral consistency here? How does an auction house decide to not sell paraphernalia from the Holocaust, "a decision which I applaud by the way," but instead decides that it's okay to sell slavery paraphernalia? I mean, is there some kind of statute of limitations on Black pain? I think not. And I don't understand this obvious incongruence in their house policy.

It adds insult to injury to tell Black folks that this really isn't an auction of slavery paraphernalia. They say it is an auction of the American Civil War Collection, which just happens to contain pieces of slavery paraphernalia. Okay, how about simply lifting the offensive artifacts from the collection prior to the auction. If there is anything I hate, it's having my intelligence insulted.

Four, this decision by Christie's is improper because it sends the wrong message—that Christie's is willing to profit from the misery of those of who were stolen, bought and sold into slavery.

Finally, it is now the job of Christie's public relations department to do what's called damage control. It is our job, I believe, to let Christie's know that with this decision they are out of control. Because yours truly is not a preferred customer on Christie's catalog mailing list, just yesterday afternoon I learned of this auction set for 10:00 a.m. tomorrow morning. I called Tom Joyner and Tom and I agreed that it was important, nonetheless, to make our loyal audience aware of this situation. I don't know what we can do in twenty-four hours between now and 10:00 a.m. tomorrow morning, but I don't put anything past our audience. On the other hand, I'm afraid to think what's going to come if we don't do something right now. And so, I'd like to make a quick motion that we share with our audience the phone number at Christie's. Get your pens. Is my motion passed? All in favor say aye. All opposed, shut up.

Here is the number to Christie's. Put it on your speed redial for today and dial it all day long until you get through to Christie's and let them know that this is absolutely racist. I don't throw the "r" word around, but when the house policy says one thing, it ought to be consistent. The phone number is (212) 546-1000. If you can't write it down right now just commit it to memory. It's in New York. Again, it's (212) 546-1000. Even at the last minute, nothing beats failure but a try, and I believe this is the right thing to do.

Afterthought: *Without question, this is the proudest moment of my tenure with the* Tom Joyner Morning Show. *Within two hours of my airing this commentary, Christie's pulled the items and later donated them to a museum as we had requested. Later still, (after another embarrassing commentary on air) the president of Christie's invited me to a meeting in her office. She later came on the radio program to apologize to our audience and to detail the changes in their house policy.*

PUBLIC POLICY

October 8, 1996

Tom Joyner Morning Show Topic: Voter Registration

Tom, I am sick of seeing the Right fight against anything that makes it easier for folks to vote. They were against the Motor Voter bill which allows folks to register to vote when they get their driver's license or renew it. They were opposed to that. They are opposed to sameday voter registration, which John Conyers Jr., the African American Congressman from Detroit, has been pushing. If you are an American and you have the documentation to prove it, why not be able to go to the polls on election day, register on the spot, and vote? The Right is still opposed to that.

I personally even like the idea of being able to vote on weekends. Many other countries do this. We've never tried it here in America, but I think we could try giving people a chance to vote on the weekends when they have more leisure time. But voting is always on Tuesdays in this country because it's tradition, and you know how we are about changing tradition. But people have to change with the times. And given the fact that we have parents who are working more than one job, families where both parents are working, single parents who don't have time to do much of anything, I think if you let people vote on the weekends when they aren't so pressed by adding yet another thing to their "to do list," we'd probably see voter turn-out go up.

But again, the Right is opposed to that. Typically, they claim that they are against these measures designed to involve more Americans in the political process because these things lead to greater voter fraud. We hear that same refrain all the time, which I think is nonsense. The fact of the matter is that when you make it easier for folks who are politically or socially or even economically disenfranchised, when you make it easier for these folks to participate in the process, it may well change the outcome of certain elections.

The Right, for example, has perfected the use of perhaps the easiest way we know to vote, and that is voting by absentee ballot. Absentee ballots can, and in fact do, change the outcome in various elections.

How many times have you watched, and mark my words, election night coverage on November 5, some reporter or campaign aide, or even a candidate who is nervous, say to the camera that the absentee ballots have not yet been counted? These ballots do make a difference.

This morning, as I talk about getting out to vote, let me mention three very quick ways that you can vote by absentee ballot. Now the rules change a little bit state to state, but basically here is what happens:

First, you can call the Elections Bureau or the County Clerk's Office, whomever the adjudicating elections authority is in your area, be it the clerk or whomever. You can call them and request an absentee ballot.

Second, if they don't respond—and they always do—you can call the party of your choice, and I know you will get a response. If you call the Republican Party, Democratic Party or the party of your choice and ask them to send you a ballot, because they want to win the election, they certainly will get one out to you right away. You can actually go to the clerk's office or go to the Elections Bureau prior to the election and cast your ballot right there on the spot. You can walk in during your lunch hour and cast your vote over the counter at the office whenever you have time to do so.

Third, in many cities and states around the country, you get what we call voter guides. This guide or voter pamphlet gives you some idea of what's on the ballot. And usually in that voter guide there is a sheet that you can either tear out, or there is information in the voter pamphlet to tell you how you can register to vote.

The point is if you have to vote by absentee ballot, then do so. We just don't want you to be absent on Election Day. The bottom line is that the Right has really perfected this art of absentee balloting. And it does in many instances make the difference in elections.

October 24, 1996

TJMS Topic: California's PROP. 209

We talked on this show about California's Proposition 209, the so-called California Civil Rights Initiative, or the CCRI; a measure that if passed on Tuesday, November 5, would eliminate affirmative action programs in public education, public employment and public contracting.

This is not just a measure in California now. It started in California, but there are now at least a dozen other states across the country who have basically copycatted this measure. To call this mean-spirited measure a civil rights initiative is an absolute affront to everything that the Movement represented. If anything, it is a civil wrongs' initiative. But to call it a civil rights initiative is an absolute bastardization of everything that Dr. King stood for.

Affirmative action has been cast as a debate of Black versus White, but if you really think about it, it's really one of wrong versus right. I mean Black folks still lag far behind White Americans in every single leading economic indicator category. So one has to ask why the fight has been cast as one of Black versus White. And the answer simply is that when you add a tinge of racism to any issue, as we all know, your chances of winning that issue in this country are a little bit better.

We all know that White women, respectfully, and not Black folks have been the greatest beneficiaries of affirmative action programs, and so I ask somewhat rhetorically whether or not the fight really ought to be between White men and White women? Just asking. Furthermore, does anyone in his or her right mind this morning really believe that affirmative action is to blame for the economic conditions which we are facing in this country?

The jobs are not going from White to Black. The jobs are going from North to South. That's the one thing that Ross Perot was right about. We've got more and more American jobs being sent south of the border. Now, as if these distortions and these deceptions about affirmative action weren't bad enough, now Republicans have crafted and are ready to deliver the ultimate insult.

They have a television commercial promoting ending affirmative action which they are about to run in the state of California, and perhaps across the country—a television commercial featuring Dr. King's "I Have a Dream" speech at the March on Washington. Even though they've pulled it, it's a good thing we are talking about this because this is the absolute brazen nature of these folks. They might as well go to Atlanta and tap dance on Dr. King's grave.

They think that Dr. King gave only one speech in his entire life, and in that one speech, he only had one line, and that is the line that he wanted his four little children to live in a nation where they would not be judged by the color of their skin but by the content of their character. So they turn this argument around and act as if because Dr. King would not want someone to be judged by the color of their skin, he then would be opposed to affirmative action, which they define as a racial preference. So they take his language and twist it all around.

Somebody tell me to pull up if I'm wrong, but I didn't see Newt Gingrich on any of the freedom rides. I didn't see Bob Dole spending the night in the Birmingham jail with Dr. King. And yet, in the name of fairness, they want to go back and pull one line out of one speech and twist it like a pretzel to act as if Dr. King, if he were around, would be opposed to affirmative action.

I've had it with these folks who are taking Dr. King's words. And we stand back and let them do this, twist his language and act as if Dr. King would be opposing a corrective program like affirmative action that's only designed to level the playing field. It is an absolute affront to Dr. King. Anyone who would sit back and even think of a television commercial like that ought to be slapped.

And this is why on election day, to bring this full circle, people have to go to the polls. Because if they will and craft a devious scheme such as this, you don't know what else they are willing to do. That's why turning out on Tuesday, November 5, is so very important to our community.

Afterthought: *When I offered this commentary, twelve states were trying to emulate California's Prop. 209. One year later, twenty-six states were attempting to qualify a similar measure on their state ballot. Frightening.*

December 12, 1996

TJMS Topic: Black Farmers

I've said before that there are no good times to be Black in America, but some times are worse than others. Yesterday, I was going through my *Tom Joyner Morning Show* files trying to locate a particular piece of material that we had discussed here one day. And while searching for what I needed, I began to note, with some interest, the number of commentaries I've offered here on the program having to do specifically with racial matters. And being the self-critic that I am—I'm the toughest critic I know on myself—I began to wonder whether or not I'd been focusing almost too much on racial matters. And so I calculated the percentage of times I'd talked about issues having to do with race. I was startled, quite frankly, by the percentage.

But then I went back through the files again and I began to review specifically what I had talked about. I talked about things like the defeat of affirmative action in California, the racial discrimination at Texaco, Avis, Circuit City, the CIA and crack cocaine in South Central L.A. and the Air Force reservists who were confronted by personnel wearing Ku Klux Klan hoods at Kelly Air Force Base in San Antonio, Texas. And now in yesterday's *Washington Post* we learn that while the number of U.S. farms that failed was 14% over a decade, from 1982 to 1992, the number of Black-owned farms that failed was 43%.

Why do Black farmers have it so hard and who, in fact, do they blame? They blame the government, the United States Department of Agriculture (USDA). It appears that bias and discrimination against Black farmers has been confirmed by agricultural officials. And in addition to having to deal with competition, agri-business, drought and flood, Black farmers apparently also have to contend with being denied loans because of what else. The color of their skin.

Blacks only make up 1% of farmers these days in this country. And the few Black farm owners who remain are being forced into bankruptcy and foreclosure because they can't get the support from their government that other farmers who happen not to be Black get much more readily.

Once again, here we see the federal government at the center of a controversy by not allowing African Americans to progress economically. In the final analysis, I went through this file one last time, and I think it finally occurred to me that it wasn't really Tavis Smiley who was focusing so much on race matters. I think we are witnessing in this country a brand new harshness the likes of which we have not seen for a long time.

What's really required on these race issues is for folks to quit putting their heads in the sand. We need a lot more dialogue about these issues and much less monologue on the issue of race. I just feel a little bit better this morning knowing that, excuse my English, it ain't me. We are witnessing again, a new harshness, a new mean-spiritedness, and racial matters are really headed in more of a downward spiral than they have in a long time, if one can actually imagine that.

January 9, 1997

TJMS Topic: Ebonics

The only thing worse than a bad idea is a bad idea replicated, so get ready for an Ebonics curriculum coming to a school district near you soon. As you all know, Ebonics is a combination of "ebony" and "phonics." The whole country's been debating it, and it seems that since the Oakland School District's decision to declare so-called Black English a language form, others around the country are now lining up willing to use taxpayers' money to train teachers to instruct African American students in their so-called "mother tongue." Or as some people call it, their "primary language."

You probably can tell by now what I think of this Ebonics debate. But I understand very clearly that the Black community is somewhat divided on this issue. Some people think it's a good idea, others think it's a bad idea. There are at least three things about this debate that I appreciate.

One, I can't recall the last time this country had a discussion or real dialogue about the need, indeed the right, the entitlement of inner-city youth, and particularly African American students, to be provided a quality education.

Two, it is not often that I find myself engaged in a debate where everybody at least wants the best for the kids involved. Whether you are for Ebonics or whether you are against it, I presume that most people who are involved in the debate or who have an opinion on it are at least taking that position because they want the best for African American students. And again, that's not something we often see in this country.

Three, you have to admit that Ebonics has made for some great comedy!

But, let me ask five questions that you may want to consider about this Ebonics debate which I still don't know the answers to. Maybe J. does, but I don't.

One, why did the Oakland School Board initially define Ebonics as "genetically based"? That's an insult. But that's how they described it.

Two, what is Black English anyway? I'm still trying to figure out what Black English is. I didn't know there was White English, Black English, Red English, J. Anthony Brown English! What the heck is Black English to begin with?

Three, correct me if I'm wrong here, but don't we pay teachers to tell the kids what they know and not the other way around?

Four, couldn't we be debating something else? Couldn't taxpayer money be spent for something better like books or teachers?

And finally, I fundamentally don't get this debate. If a kid walks into a classroom and starts splitting verbs, busting infinitives is speaking improper English. Correct him. Again, why are we even in this debate about Ebonics? If it's wrong, it's wrong. Correct the kid in a sensitive and straightforward way and let's move on. That's what worked for us and I don't know why it won't work for kids today. I just don't understand this debate at its basic and core level.

Afterthought: *I still don't get it!*

February 20, 1997

TJMS Topic: Black Voting Rights?

You know, Sybil and I actually talked about this a couple of weeks ago and apparently there is either something in the water or something on the Internet or both regarding the Voting Rights Act of 1965 because we have received so much mail and so many phone calls. Let me try to clear this up the best that I can. I did a little research on this and I want to set the record straight for those who are concerned about it and may have read about it on the Internet.

First of all, since this is Black History Month, here's a quick bit of history: the Voting Rights Act of 1965 was passed by Congress and gave African Americans the right to vote as statutory law and not as a constitutional amendment. Those are two different things. Of course, there were constitutional amendments that first granted the right to vote. For example, the fiftieth Amendment passed in 1870 first granted the right to vote to African American men only. And years later, women were granted the right to vote in 1920 with the passage of the women's suffrage bill.

The Voting Rights Act of 1965 removed many of the barriers like poll taxes and literacy tests that kept many African Americans from voting, particularly down in the South. This was applied to states where there was a history of voter disenfranchisement, especially in most southern states and even some northern jurisdictions like New York City and Chicago, where lawsuits were filed.

Now, as I said a moment ago, the Act was originally passed to remain in effect as a statutory law. It was to remain in effect for twenty years and every twenty years, of course, Congress had to renew the Act. The last time the Voting Rights Act was approved for another twenty-year cycle was during the Reagan Administration back in the mid-1980s. It was extended for twenty years until the year 2007, which people have been hearing and reading about on the Internet.

Now the controversy has to do with whether or not it gets renewed. Does it have to be ratified by thirty-eight states or ratified by another vote of Congress? It is the latter. We do not have to go back through the process of trying to get thirty-eight states to ratify it. That may be an impossibility. But the fact of the matter is that Congress will actually vote on this issue. The answer to the question, of what people can do at this point (as we've been talking about for the last year on the *Tom Joyner Morning Show*) is to make sure that between now and 2007 everybody you vote for, particularly those who you send to Congress, supports renewal of the Voting Rights Act. That's the way it has to be done. So it is, in fact, Congress who votes to ratify this act and not the states. I wanted to take a moment at least to clear that up.

Why is this more an issue for African Americans in particular rather than all other Americans? I know you aren't ready for this, but probably because we're Black. That may have a little something to do with it.

> **Afterthought:** *Without question this is the most misunderstood public policy issue I've addressed on the* Tom Joyner Morning Show. *Everybody seemed to think that their right to vote was about to be taken away. Tom wanted me to clear up the confusion. I've never seen so many people who don't exercise their right to vote get so upset that the right might be taken away. Go figure.*

April 8, 1997

TJMS Topic: Magic, AIDS and the Black Community

I want to talk a few minutes about the recent cover of *Ebony* magazine. Those of you who have seen the most recent issue of the magazine know that Earvin "Magic" Johnson and his wife, Cookie, are featured on the cover in an exclusive story in which they declare that Magic has been healed of the HIV virus that causes AIDS. Magic and Cookie testified that God has cured Magic from the virus which abruptly ended his stellar N.B.A. career with the Los Angeles Lakers. Now Magic's doctors were very quick to point out that while the HIV virus is essentially undetectable in Magic's blood, this ought not to be confused with the virus necessarily being absent from his body altogether.

I am no doctor, but some of us do know what a little faith in God can accomplish. The Bible says that faith the size of a grain of a mustard seed can move mountains. I happen to know that to be true. And if, in fact, God has healed Magic Johnson, then Magic really has no choice but to give God the glory as he and Cookie do in this most recent issue of *Ebony*.

On the other hand, we all know quite well that Magic's financial resources have permitted him the luxury of being able to work with people like Dr. David Ho who was *Time* magazine's Man-of-the-Year last year for all the advances and discoveries that he has made working with the AIDS virus. Magic has been treated by Dr. David Ho and other individuals who are on the cutting edge of the most promising treatments available for HIV and AIDS.

Many, however, don't have the economic resources of Magic Johnson. Quite frankly, this means access to quality healthcare for most people infected with HIV and AIDS. Treatment and quality healthcare is still nothing more than a pipe dream for many. Magic's access and response to new medication underscores the need to pick up the pace on AIDS research and not grow weary of the conversation about AIDS as so many of us have become.

Last night when we talked about this on our show on *BET*, and for that matter any time you hear discussion about AIDS, I wondered why so many people are so tuned out to listening to the conversation. They just automatically turn the channel, or flip the page, or what have you. But now, given how Magic's body has responded to this medication, we ought to be picking up the pace rather than growing weary. Especially given the fact that Black women represent the new group that AIDS is hitting at an unprecedented rate.

Yesterday, President Clinton nominated Sandy Thurman, a long time AIDS activist, to be his new AIDS advisor. I don't know Ms. Thurman, but if you look at today's paper or watched the news yesterday or today, you will notice that Ms. Thurman happens to be a blonde, White woman. I say that not because I want to cast any aspersion on her, she's a long-time AIDS activist, and from what I understand, she's qualified to be in the position. I only raise the issue because at a time when AIDS is becoming more and more a Black thing, particularly for Black women, we need to be expanding the diversity of AIDS leadership to target those people who are being most affected. The White House and those in the AIDS community are challenged to make sure that we expand and have a multifaceted approach to deal with the virus and the new community that it is affecting and infecting. We need more diversity and more money for research. We need to not grow weary of this conversation.

We need to do everything we can to find the cure to this deadly disease. Ultimately, we need to recognize who this AIDS virus is now starting to prey upon and to do everything in our power to make sure that Black folks and others, particularly African American women, are educated about the dangers that lurk with regard to HIV and AIDS.

Magic has done us all a favor by again putting this story on the front page. Now the time has come again to pay attention and do what we ought to be doing to curb the spread of this deadly disease.

Afterthought: *I received more than a few pieces of mail from listeners who thought I was questioning the healing power of God Almighty. I thought my commentary was pretty clear about my faith in God...but I've learned that people sometimes hear things that were never said.*

April 10, 1997

TJMS Topic: Prop. 209 and the Story behind the Story

You know by now that a federal appeals court reversed a lower court injunction that had blocked enforcement of the initiative of Prop. 209, which the voters passed in California. California voters, as far as I'm concerned, effectively let down the country when they voted for that initiative.

As I've said before, what happens in California politics can either cast a very long shadow, or a long sunbeam. This is a matter that affects and ought to concern all of us across the country whether you live in California or not. In fact, at least a dozen other states are now moving as quickly as they can to qualify the same kind of measure that we saw the federal appeals court support in the state of California.

I'm not going to spend my time this morning talking about it. I think those who listen to the show on a daily basis know exactly how I feel about affirmative action. It is still, in my judgment, a corrective program that works. It is a corrective program that is designed to balance unequal scales. We do not live in a color-blind society and I'm tired of affirmative action being scapegoated because of the economic angst of so-called angry White men.

No one is going to believe that the jobs are going from White people to Black people. That's absolute nonsense. There are no numbers anywhere which suggest that jobs are going from White to Black. The jobs may be going from North to South, that is to say that more and more American corporations are posting record profits here at home and sending more American jobs abroad. So if you happen to be, respectfully, an angry White male, your job may very well be in Indonesia, Philippines or in Taiwan, but it sure ain't on the South Side of Chicago, in South Central Los Angeles or in West Philly. That is not where you will find your job. As I said, I really don't want to spend my time talking about affirmative action. What I do want to talk about is what I call the story behind the story.

We know that the real story, on the surface, is that the injunction was reversed. What you may not know though is that there was a judge whose name is Thelton Henderson. He is the Chief U.S. District Judge in San Francisco who ordered the implementation of the injunction against this proposition. The judge stepped in and ordered an injunction. Thelton Henderson is African American and a Democrat appointed by Jimmy Carter. When the appeals court sat this week to reverse this decision, can you guess who those judges were? As you may know, it's a three-member federal bench. Right now there are three White men—two appointed by Ronald Reagan, one appointed by George Bush. In a very real way, this was almost expected. When you see a federal judge appointed by Jimmy Carter, you've got a good sense of where he stands on affirmative action. And when you see judges appointed during the twelve years of Reagan and Bush, you pretty much know where they stand. What's the point? The point is, as we've said a thousand times, you can throw almost any issue at us and I can show you somewhere how that issue is linked to being involved directly in the process.

When you let people like Ronald Reagan and George Bush get elected, guess what happens? They stack the federal bench with conservative jurists. After twelve years of that, if you are forced to go to the court to get some recompense and some justice, nine times out of ten you will have to deal with a conservative judge. President Clinton has a group of federal appointees to sit on the bench that he has already submitted to the United States Senate and they are sitting on those nominations. The Republican controlled Senate is letting time go by before having hearings to give these judges a chance to sit on the bench.

The bottom line is that it all goes back to being involved in the process. You asked why it was so important to vote in November, to re-elect a Democratic president, to not let the Republicans control Congress? This is the answer. The brother did everything he could. He put the injunction in, but when he was overruled, what can you say about it? It all starts with us. That's the bottom line.

April 22, 1997

TJMS Topic: Conservatives Propose Mandating Volunteerism in Public Housing

Once again the conservatives in Congress are out of control. The House Banking Committee is working on a massive rewrite that would overhaul federal housing as we know it. The federal government now funds about 3,400 public authorities that own and operate roughly 13,000 public housing developments across the country that shelter about 4.3 million low-income Americans at a cost of about $2.8 billion a year. So it's a massive program.

I think anybody who has been to a housing project or anybody who lives in a housing project every day, understands the need for public housing to be revamped. Issues of crime, deterioration, and other issues need to be addressed. You look at what happened to Girl X in Chicago and other examples of horrendous acts that have occurred in housing projects across the country. Clearly, the issues need to be addressed.

Now as usual, the Republicans are pushing the envelope by insisting, as part of this legislation, that all public housing tenants be required to perform eight hours of community service each month. By the way, President Clinton is expected to sign this bill whenever it gets to his desk, and it is expected to hit the floor of Congress sometime in early May 1997.

Our friend Jesse Jackson, Jr., the congressman from the Second District in Illinois, is trying to hold the dam on the banking committee against this ridiculous proposal. However, the Republicans want to insist on this provision. This at a fundamental level, is just outright demeaning. It's absolutely demeaning. To demand as part of their rent that somebody who lives in public housing do eight hours of community service a month? I'm not opposed to volunteerism. As a matter of fact, if you've seen this weeks issue of *Newsweek*, Colin Powell is on the cover talking about a plan being undertaken across the country to increase volunteerism. So nobody can be opposed to volunteerism. However, just because you receive a government subsidy, that ought not make you required to do eight hours a month. We don't make farmers do it. We don't make ranchers do it, and we certainly don't make big corporations do it. Right now, we are talking about a bailout of the tobacco industry by giving them immunity in order to avoid future lawsuits—despite the fact that all these years they have lied to Congress and the American public about what smoking does to your health.

And so we give subsidies to everybody all day long and nobody from big business is mandated to do any time with regard to community service. As usual, we want to dump on those persons who are the least among us, those on the bottom rung, those who live in public housing. Again, none of us ought to be opposed to volunteerism. In fact, I think the African American community has a pretty good record of doing volunteer activities in and outside of our community.

This is kind of an interesting segue. An organization called Independent Sector puts out a study every year or two that talks about who gives the most money to charitable organizations. It's African Americans and you know why? Because we give so much money to Black churches. We consistently rank at the top of those communities who give the most charitable contributions.

Black folks give their money, they volunteer, and we can increase that because the problems in our community suggest, quite frankly, that we have to give. However, demanding and insisting that only folks in public housing receiving government subsidies do community service is a ridiculous notion. The conservatives ought to let this thing go and the President ought not to sign this bill if it has that ridiculous measure in it. And kudos to Jesse Jackson, Jr., and Congressman Mel Watt, on the House Banking Committee, who tried to stop this provision. It looks like they may lose this battle, but they are fighting against it.

It makes no sense. Volunteerism really ought to be, in fact, voluntary. You can't make folks be volunteers. Conservatives use that argument all the time against the President's AmeriCorp program, which is his national service program. It gives college students a chance to earn money while they are in college. They repay that money by working for any number of community service organizations once they graduate.

Every year at budget time, the conservatives always argue against the President's AmeriCorp program by saying you can't pay people to volunteer. Now that argument mysteriously has gone out the window when it comes to debating why people who live in public housing projects have to volunteer their time in a mandated sort of way. It's a ridiculous notion.

August 21, 1997

TJMS Topic: Back-to-School

It's back-to-school time across the country, and you can almost hear the collective sigh of relief from parents as the summer draws to a close. My parents always seemed happier to send us back to school than we were to be reunited with friends. Then again, of course, there are ten kids in my family. If you're anything like my parents, you too are no doubt eager to hear the school bell ring. What you may not be so eager to hear is that there is yet another national debate about how to best educate America's school children. On the one side are conservative groups like the Christian Coalition and the Family Research Council. On the other side, most African American educators, advocates and the Department of Education.

The question, really, is an old question with a new twist. Should there be a national education examination to help track the academic achievement, or the lack thereof, of America's children? The new twist: should the federal government, for the first time, set those academic standards by which to judge the students' performance? As the little kids end vacation and return to the classrooms, the big kids end their recess and return to Capitol Hill to begin a debate on whether or not fourth graders should take a voluntary national test in reading, and whether eighth graders should do the same in math. As usual, conservatives are arguing state's rights again. Let the states do everything. Who cares about drawing national conclusions about the quality of our schools. What's right and what's wrong, what's working and what's not? Let the states handle it. Ever get the feeling that no matter what you ask a political conservative, the answer is always going to be let the states do it.

African American educators and advocates strongly support the momentum toward national rather that state education standards for every child. They believe, as do I, that our children in the inner city can meet these standards if they have the same resources and the same expectations. The same high expectations, I should say, as their privileged White counterparts.

Now some states are already saying they are not going to use the voluntary tests, but many big school district superintendents want their students to take the same tests as students in other states take. They want to make sure that the tests also are ethnically, culturally and linguistically diverse. But the problem is that the rules have not been set as to how they will be used in terms of retention in grade, group tracking, and graduation.

The department needs to be pressed to make sure they are ethnically and culturally diverse, and that they are not going to be used to hold students back. Now having said that, I believe that African American educators know best how to educate our children. Well, maybe not in Oakland. Seriously, I do believe that African American educators know best how to educate our students. Particularly, an organization called the National Urban Coalition. They have a program called "Say Yes to a Youngster's Future" that operates in big cities across the country and really does offer culturally affirmative, historically accurate educational opportunities to help young people lead us into the next millennium.

I just wanted to share this information as the debate heats up in the coming days and weeks in Washington, with those who listen to the program, who are in education, and those of you who are concerned parents. You may want to contact this national Black organization to get involved in making sure that we have these national standards to help our kids lead us into the next millennium.

By the way, the phone number at the National Urban Coalition is: (800) 328-6339. We've got to do everything we can in our community to make sure our kids get a chance to succeed, and we've got to make sure that we are on the right side of this particular issue.

Afterthought: *I usually have a good sense, I think, of where Black America generally stands on most issues I discuss on air. My radar was off a bit on national standards. There are significant numbers of Black educators on both sides of this issue.*

August 28, 1997

TJMS Topic: Prop. 209: Coming to a State Near You!

Tom, we started off the week on a high note. As a matter of fact, I think people all over the country are still feeling good about our ability to have a tremendous impact on helping bring back the TV show *Living Single.* And we got no props, but we'll give ourselves props, we know what we did. So we started this week on a high note, and I hate the fact that I have to end this week on a not-so-high note. Today California becomes the first state in the country to actually ban all forms of affirmative action. I've talked about this so many times. The measure, the so-called California Civil Rights Initiative, Prop. 209, actually goes into effect this morning in the state of California.

I'm almost ashamed to tell people that I live in California, given what we did on this particular issue. The numbers tell the story here and you know the numbers are abysmal. In the University of California system, admissions are down for Black students some 23%. At the University of California at San Diego, where President Clinton, by the way, gave his race relations speech, two hundred Black folks applied to medical school and not a single one got admitted. At the University of California at Berkeley's Boalt School of Law, the enrollment of Black students is down 81%. That's one of the most prestigious law schools in the country (by the way, Supreme Court Chief Justice William Rehnquist went to Boalt). There is only one Black student in the Fall class. The University of Texas system was down 26% in the admissions of Black students, and I can go on and on. The numbers here really tell the story.

The Prop. 209 case is being appealed to the Supreme Court. Unfortunately, as I told you a few weeks ago, I read in *Jet* magazine (you know I believe everything I read in *Jet*) that Clarence Thomas already told us that God told him to vote against affirmative action. So we already know what's going to happen with Clarence Thomas's vote when it gets to the Supreme Court.

I think I'm going to start giving out an award, here in the near future. I'll call it the Toby Award. You've heard of the Tony Award? This is the Toby Award. You all remember Toby? Clarence Thomas is going to be the first recipient. It's a shame that when this thing reaches the Supreme Court we are going to have to rely on the swing vote of a White woman named Sandra Day O'Connor when there is a brother sitting on the court. Whoever thought we'd live in a time when there would be a Black man sitting on the court and we would be looking for a White woman to give us her vote to save a program like affirmative action. It's ridiculous. I've said before there are no good times to be a Black person in America, but some times are worse than others.

This is a fight that we cannot run from. Dr. King said, "Cowardice asks is it safe, expediency asks is it politic, vanity asks is it popular, but conscience asks is it right? Sometimes we must take a position that is neither safe, nor comfortable, nor convenient, but we must do so because our conscience tells us it's right."

The message of this is that if it happened in California, it's coming to a state near you soon. Please do not lose this important issue by the margin of your absence at the polls. Just because it happened in California doesn't mean it has to happen in your state.

October 2, 1997

TJMS Topic: The 2000 Census Revisited

A few weeks ago, you may recall, I told you about the petty and peculiar partisan politics the Republicans are playing with the 2000 census. I promised you I would stay on top of this important issue, and I want to report this morning on some developments that have happened of late, since we last talked about it. At issue, you may remember, is how the 2000 census is going to be conducted. Modern scientific statistical computer sampling techniques are now available to us, and ought to be used to supplement the traditional headcount. Such an approach would ensure greater accuracy in the

Census Bureau's effort to count all Americans.

But since the Republicans aren't interested in accuracy but rather political gain, they have been and continue to be adamantly opposed to using the best of what modern science and technology has to offer us. Why? Because at stake is the potential loss of up to twenty-four Republican seats in the House alone. The headcounts tend to favor married homeowners who live in the suburbs, the traditional Republican base. You know that when the census is conducted every ten years, there is always a severe undercount. And you also know who gets undercounted—Black folks, people of color, immigrants, poor people, and children. I told you how especially tight the census is on brothers. Because one week he's at his Momma's house, the next week he's at his baby Momma house, next week he's living with his boys for a minute. Unfortunately, a lot of brothers happen to be on lockdown right when the census is being taken. Ultimately, when we get undercounted, we get underrepresented and underpaid since the census results are also used to divvy up your and my federal tax dollars.

In terms of connecting the dots, I also told you that a significant undercount coupled with the potential passage of this so-called Tiger Woods Bill, which again if passed, would allow folks to check a multiracial box, would further dilute Black representation and political clout. It could get ugly on Black folks in the coming years.

Enter the Republicans trying to be slick by converting what should be a vote on how to conduct the census into a vote to consult the courts as to the constitutionality of this issue before they take the step. The truth is this issue may not even make it to the courts. Here you have the Congressional Research Service telling members of Congress that in all likelihood the courts probably won't even hear this case.

For that matter, there was a case similar to this during the Bush years, and you know how conservative the courts were during the Bush years. They wouldn't even hear it. They didn't tell the Republicans what they wanted to hear even back during the Bush era. But never let facts, never let good information, get in the way of trying to dis Black people. So they want to move this issue to the courts, let the courts make a decision on it. And we ultimately know that the preparation and the research required to go into court to argue this case takes time. You know how backed up the court system is. The plan is to put this thing in the court system and to never get to it until far after the census in the year 2000.

I think the bottom line is that we ought to respectfully challenge the President to get out front on this issue. We must use all the scientific and technological advances that we've made to have as accurate a count as possible. Whoever that group was that counted the Million Man March, we don't want them. This is about long-term representation, long-term political clout, and the access to resources that the Black community will have or not have ten years into a new millennium.

The President ought to put the Republicans on notice and confront them on this issue. The Congressional Black Caucus should speak out more forcefully on this, to let Black folks and the country know what's happening. This is not about an accurate count, it's about the Republicans playing politics. And finally, this again underscores to our listening audience how important it is to go to the polls, to participate in the process, and most important, to elect good quality officials. Because sometimes, whether we like it or not, we get to a place where the situation is really out of our hands. Even though we are the voters and they are working for us, it gets to a point where these deals are done in the back room. And unless we have somebody there representing our interests, we get screwed every time. Here is a case where we see them about to kick us in the behind, quite frankly.

October 23, 1997

TJMS Topic: Just Do It!

In a recent speech President Bill Clinton declared "The Senate's failure to act on my nominations or even give my nominees a hearing represents the worst of partisan politics." No truer words have ever been uttered by our friend Bill Clinton. Close to one hundred federal judgeships sit vacant as we speak. This is primarily because the U.S. Senate, which must confirm these nominations, is resisting, outright defying the President's formal power—indeed his constitutional responsibility—to fill these positions.

Because a majority of states are run by Republican governors, state courts, stacked with ideologically conservative Republican appointed jurists, have become almost openly hostile to important social issues on the African American agenda. And so Black folks have found themselves being forced increasingly to appeal to federal courts to find any justice. You will recall sometime back that I talked about a progressive Black federal judge in California, Judge Thelton Henderson, who was at the right place, at the right time, and put in the injunction-stopping implementation of that crazy Prop. 209. And so that was a rare occasion, but more often than not we find no refuge even in federal court because Reagan and Bush during their twelve years of political tyranny stacked the federal judiciary with all their conservative cronies. Now that there is a new sheriff in town trying to deputize some new troops, the Republican Senate is resisting what they call the "Clintonization" of the federal bench.

They complain, as usual, that the President is nominating his friends and supporters in some cases. What is he supposed to do, nominate enemies and opponents? I mean, please! The President's nominees to date have received higher ratings from the American Bar Association on average than the Reagan/Bush appointees, and to his credit, Clinton has appointed more Black and female judges than Reagan and Bush combined. As you will recall from your high school government classes—go back with me Sybil, in your case Tom and J. go way back—the legislative branch of government writes the law, the executive branch signs the law, but the judicial branch interprets the law.

Fundamentally, you can write and pass all the legislation you want, but if in the final stage, the Reagan and Bush federal judiciary can issue its conservative interpretation, what have we really accomplished? I say it's time for the Clinton Administration to declare war on the pompous Republican Senate and let the American people know what kind of partisan political games are being played here. Now is no time for conjecture, it's time to challenge. I mean some of these right-wing ideologues on the Hill have gone beyond the simple nonsense of not wanting to hold hearings for these nominees, to talking openly about impeachment hearings against "liberal" judges whose rulings go against "the will of the people." What people? I'm part of that "we the people," and I don't have a problem with what Judge Henderson did.

I saw the President this morning out jogging

on my way to the the D.C. studio. He had his headset on and was laughing so hard, I know he was listening to us this morning. Mr. President, with all due respect, sir, you need to go on the offensive. Have your people read Article 2, Section 2. Do the sneak attack move and appoint a coterie of progressive federal judges when the Senate goes on recess, November 14.

Mr. President, even Jeffrey Dahmer and Timothy McVeigh had a hearing.

November 6, 1997

TJMS Topic: What a Difference a Day Makes

On Tuesday morning, we were asking, begging folks to give anybody and everybody they knew in Houston a wake-up call to remind them that Tuesday was Election Day and the eyes of the country were on the city of Houston. I'm so glad that our friends in Houston didn't hit the snooze button and sleep right on through our wake-up call. Instead, there was a heavy turnout in Houston, even in the Black community. And the ballot measure to repeal affirmative action, which would have made Houston the first city to do so, went down to defeat. Thank God.

Now because political victories for Black folks these days are about as common as a sighting of Haley's Comet, one would love to first thank the city of Houston for casting that long sunbeam, instead a long shadow, and then pass out cigars and Cristal, or Dom Perignon if you prefer and get our party on for a minute. Tempted as we may be to celebrate and get our backyard boogie on for just a minute, I'm reminded of the words of the late great Dr. Benjamin Elijah

Mays who once said:

I have only just a minute
Only sixty seconds in it
Forced upon me—can't refuse it
Didn't seek it, didn't choose it
But it's up to me to use it
I must suffer if I lose it
Give account if I abuse it
Just a tiny little minute
But eternity is in it.

And so the words of Dr. Mays challenge us this morning to consider what we really ought to be doing in this particular minute. And so we look around, and while we could celebrate what happened in one city Tuesday, we consider what could happen to our country today.

This morning, right here in Washington, two votes, not one, two votes threaten to escalate the attack on affirmative action. What a difference a day makes. And it's really a double whammy. These Capitol Hill conservatives know how they intend to spend their minutes this morning. They are hitting us high and low. They are hitting us from the left, from the right, from the Senate side and the House side. At 9:30 this morning in the House, HR 1909, the so-called Canady Bill, is being voted on in the House Judiciary Committee. If passed, HR 1909, the so-called Civil Rights Act of 1997, patterned after Proposition 209 in California, will prohibit the entire federal government from engaging in affirmative action. Forget a city, we're talking about the entire country here. We are talking federal law, education, employment, contracting, grants and every other federal activity. That's in the House at 9:30 a. m.

Across the hall in the Senate Judiciary Committee, just a half an hour later, at ten o'clock, it appears that Bill Lee, President Clinton's choice for the nation's top civil rights job, is about to crash and burn. Republicans who control the committee have made it quite clear from the chairman on down, that they intend to block Lee's nomination for Assistant Attorney General for Civil Rights. Why? Did he lie, cheat, embezzle? No, his crime is that he supports affirmative action. Plain and simple. Bill Lee has spent two decades as an attorney for the NAACP Legal Defense and Education Fund. Not a question, not a hint about his integrity has been raised. This is unconscionable. It is untenable that a few senators can block the nomination of someone who does not have a blemish on his record, simply because he believes in affirmative action. But that's what is happening in the Senate at ten o'clock. And so the battle continues.

Finally, if you happen to be here in the nation's capital at 9:30 this morning, please, if you are anywhere near the Hill, make your way to the Rayburn House office building at 9:30 for that Judiciary Committee meeting. If you're in your car right now and you are close to the Hill, stop by a rally that's happening, that's being led by the Congressional Black Caucus at 2128 in the Rayburn House office building. But certainly at 9:30 go to that committee meeting and let your presence make a statement if you are anywhere near the Capital.

These actions by the House and the Senate are absolutely unacceptable. And so the battle goes on.

Afterthought: *Apparently a lot of listeners were near the Hill that morning! A few days later we were joined on the* Tom Joyner Morning Show *by Congressional Black Caucus Chairwoman Maxine Waters who thanked our audience for showing up at the House Judiciary Committee meeting. Just in case you were wondering, HR1909 never passed out of Committee. (Smile)*

February 5, 1998

TJMS Topic: The Death Penalty is Wrong!

By now, Tom, you and the rest of the audience now know that Carla Fay Tucker was executed by lethal injection in Texas. Where else? This was the first woman to be put to death in that state since the Civil War.

By now you also know where I stand on the death penalty. It is wrong. The death penalty does not serve as a deterrent. The death penalty is not redemptive. It does not bring back your loved one. The death penalty is fatal and final. If we had performed executions, what could we have said to the families of any one of the seventy-two persons to date that have been released from death row because they were falsely accused? My bad? The death penalty is applied unfairly. The electric chair; it's the one time a brother is guaranteed a reserved seat. However, this was not the execution of a brother, but a White woman.

Some might cynically ask why I care about a White woman being executed. That's simple. As the song says, "Red, Yellow, Black or White, all life is precious in His sight." But there are other reasons why I care. I care because we are told that the goal of incarceration is rehabilitation. The Carla Fay Tucker who was profiled on *60 Minutes* and *CNN*, and for that matter everywhere else, was indeed a changed person. Her sincere religious conversion and her good work during her more than fourteen years in prison attest to that. Indeed she married by proxy, in 1995, a prison ministry worker. I care because a brother of one the victims asked that her death sentence be commuted. Genuine remorse, rehabilitation, a sincere spiritual conversion, marriage to a prison minister, and a brother of one of the victims asking for her death sentence to be commuted, and yet the Board of Pardons and Parole voted sixteen to zero against the request by these individuals that her death sentence be exchanged for life without the possibility of parole. That decision in part came, as you know, because in the state of Texas there is no such sentence. There is no life without parole in Texas—there is just no life.

So what are we saying here? A couple of things quickly. One, there are several Black women who sit on death row. I don't mean to be crass, but if they can execute a White woman who had the Pope and Pat Robertson pleading on her behalf, what then becomes of these sisters who sit on death row? And God knows, a brother is in a hard spot this morning, most especially if you're in Texas.

But it also raises another issue. Will *60 Minutes*, *CNN*, and all the other media outlets start doing profiles on these sisters when their time comes up to be executed?

Finally, the Pope is consistently opposed to the death penalty. Pat Robertson of the religious Right is consistently pro-death penalty. One has to wonder this morning, why Pat Robertson, Jerry Falwell and other ministers on the Right had their own conversion in this particular case. I'll leave that one for you to ponder.

February 10, 1998

TJMS Topic: Ronald Reagan Washington National Airport

Tom, this Friday for our Valentine's Day show, you and the crew will be flying into the newly remodeled and newly renamed Ronald Reagan Washington National Airport. That's right, just in time for his eighty-seventh birthday Congressional Republicans voted to rename Washington National after the former President. President Clinton, in no position to pick a fight with the Right, quickly signed the legislation. Now you'll forgive me this morning if I seem less than exuberant about singing happy birthday to Ronald Reagan. I guess I keep remembering how he and the Republicans fought tooth and nail to keep Dr. King's birthday from becoming a federal holiday (so the nation could sing happy birthday to Martin).

But I'm not here this morning to beat up on Ronald Reagan, although he did beat us down for eight years. Remember Reaganomics? *Supply side* and *trickle down* during the "greed is good" decade of the '80s? There was never any supply on our side, and nothing ever trickled down. But here again, I'm not here to beat up on Ronald Reagan. "A rising tide will lift all boats." Yeah, if you have a boat. "Pull yourself up by your bootstraps." But what if you don't have any boots and you're standing in quicksand? But here again, I'm not here this morning to beat up on Ronald Reagan.

A man who only had one Black in his cabinet, Samuel Pierce—one Black in the whole cabinet. And once in a receiving line at the White House, Reagan didn't know who Secretary Pierce was. But I'm not here to beat up on Ronald Reagan.

For my money, Jesse Jackson still has the best line on Ronald Reagan. Remember the 1984 Democratic National Convention, when the Reverend Jackson said, "I'd rather have Roosevelt in a wheelchair than Reagan on a horse." Since we're not here to beat up on Ronald Reagan this morning, I won't do that. But I do have a few issues with the folks in Congress who started this mess.

For starters, the name, Ronald Reagan Washington National Airport is just too long. If you've ever spent any time in Los Angeles, you no doubt have traveled the 10 Freeway. You almost have to, to go to certain places. A few years back, one state legislator in California who clearly had way too much time on his hands decided we should rename the 10 Freeway the Christopher Columbus Transcontinental Highway.

And you know what? This may shock you, but we still call it the 10! I suspect the Ronald Reagan Washington National Airport will still be called National. Second, National Airport is already named after one president, our first, George Washington. Are we going to play the father of our country like that? What's next, the Ronald Reagan Washington Monument? Overkill people, overkill.

Third, this is just another example of how the folks who live and work in Washington get dissed by the federal government all the time. Taxation without representation. Ronald Reagan hails, as I said, from California, and I'd be kicking up all kinds of sand if I was told by folks I did not elect that the airport in my city, LAX, would be changed to the Ronald Reagan Los Angeles International Airport. Finally, since Congress seems to be gung ho about changing the names of buildings here in Washington to honor great Americans, how about the Ronald H. Brown Department of Commerce?

RACE & RACISM

January 16, 1997

Tom Joyner Morning Show Topic: The Confederate Flag

You know, Tom, it's not often that I have anything good to say about the political Right. In fact, I never have anything good to say about right-wing conservatives, most primarily because they almost never do the right thing. Which is why you always hear me refer to the political Right as the half-Right. They always tell you half the truth, give you half the facts, tell you half the story, and never see more than half the picture.

Today though, it must be a cold day you-know-where and the moon may very well have a blue tint to it tonight because "every now and then," as the old gospel spiritual declares, somebody on the half-Right has the courage to tell the whole truth. And when they do, although rarely, I think it's necessary, indeed mandatory, that we acknowledge their enlightenment. And so, today, I'd like to speak very briefly about the Republican Governor of South Carolina, a guy named David Beasley, who has staked his entire political career on his effort to remove the confederate flag from atop the state capitol in Columbia, South Carolina. The Governor promised when he ran for office a couple of years back that he would keep the flag flying, but once he got in office he created a race relations commission. Subsequently he has decided, based on the advice of the commission, to remove this divisive symbol from atop the capitol. Now as Black folks, and I'm not going to belabor the point here, we know what the confederate flag means to us—nothing. But a whole lot of White folks in South Carolina who voted for Governor Beasley, as you can imagine, ain't exactly laughing, especially the so-called Christian conservatives (isn't that an oxymoron).

Check this out, one Republican state legislator urged one of his colleagues who announced her support for the Governor's position to "quickly get qualified for a federal witness protection program." That's ugly and how serious this fight in South Carolina has become. Quotes like that are not exactly what I'd call *hidden* racism.

As I said a moment ago, very rarely does someone on the Right have the courage to stand up and do the right thing. For Black folks in South Carolina for those of us who have relatives there, which I guess means all the rest of us, we need to let the Governor of South Carolina know that we support his effort to get the conservative flag off the state capitol. I guess there is hope for all of us, because guess who has gotten in line to support the Governor's decision in South Carolina? Believe it or not, Senator Strom Thurmond! So it really must be a cold, cold, cold day you-know-where!

Afterthought: *The only commentary in this book giving props to the political Right. I hope you enjoyed it! It's also the shortest commentary in the book!*

March 13, 1997

TJMS Topic: Sex, Race and the Army

As you know, so often in the Black community, we will raise hell about something for a minute or two and then a week or two later, we've forgotten about what happened and we're not riding the issue the way we ought to ride it. Well, this week the NAACP and Mr. Mfume had a press conference along with the five White women who allegedly had sex with or were raped by Army soldiers at the Aberdeen Proving Ground—which is just north of Baltimore— . These women had alleged earlier that they were raped by some military officers.

There are thirteen servicemen in the Army who have been charged with sexual misconduct. Of the thirteen, seven are Black. And of the thirteen, only seven have been criminally charged. And it just so happens—I know you will find this hard to believe—that the seven who have been criminally charged are all African Americans. The women came out originally and said they were raped. At the press conference this week, we found out that they were, in fact, verbally abused and pressured to cooperate with the investigation. In fact, they were promised immunity from prosecution if they cooperated. During the press conference, the women admitted to having consensual sex with the officers and that they were not in fact forced or raped.

Yesterday, Togo West, who is the Secretary of the Army and the highest ranking Black man in the Army, had a meeting with the Congressional Black Caucus and Mr. Kweisi Mfume of the NAACP. Togo West's comments in the paper today really suggest that he does not believe that these five White women were coerced, or that they were pressured in any way to offer their statements. So you can see the divide that is now starting to widen.

Mr. Mfume and Mr. West had to respectfully disagree on where they stood on this issue. But it sets up an interesting paradox. You have the highest ranking Black man in the Army saying he doesn't believe these women were forced into anything. And you've got seven Black men of thirteen people involved who happen to be the only individuals criminally charged. They, of course, are wondering what's going to happen to their careers, because these women have now come out and said that they were in fact forced to make these statements.

So it sets up an interesting paradox between one Black man and seven other Black men and where this story is going to go we don't know. However, it is worth talking about because the NAACP and Black America, need to stay on top of this story and make sure that this kind of behavior doesn't go unchecked. Another African American, Sergeant Major Gene McKinney, the highest ranking enlisted man in the Army, also had a White woman accuse him of sexual misconduct. He is sitting on the sideline while he is being investigated. So this is not something that just happened at the Aberdeen military base, it happens across the country. It's widespread in the military and something has to be done about it. Here is the best opportunity for us to do something about it. The NAACP and other African American organizations and leaders, including the Congressional Black Caucus, ought not to let this thing die on the vine.

Why would the White women change their story? It's a legitimate question and one of the reasons why it's an important question is because not only would it be easier for them to stick to their story, but it would be more advantageous. They do not know at this point whether or not they are still going to be protected from prosecution now that they have come forth. These five White women took a giant step to recant their story, and now they may be prosecuted as a result of it.

They've essentially come out and admitted to having sex with their instructors which is a violation of Army policy. So the question before the Army now is, do they continue to offer these women protection from immunity as they promised initially, or now that they have come out and recanted their story, should they be prosecuted for having violated Army policy by having sex with these officers?

Afterthought: *Sergeant Major Gene McKinney is now the former highest ranking man in the Army. He awaits a jury verdict on his alleged sexual misconduct involving a number of women as I write this notation. This just in: Mr McKinney has been acquitted of all but one of nineteen counts against him. He was convicted of obstructing justice. Initially facing a maximum sentence of fifty-five years if found guilty of all charges, he now faces a maximum of five years for the one guilty verdict.*

April 24, 1997

TJMS Topic: Fuzzy's Apology

Tom, I'm sure everybody is familiar with the discriminatory remarks made by White professional golfer Fuzzy Zoeller about Master's champion Tiger Woods by now. You know the "little boy" reference followed by the "fried chicken and collard greens" insult. Zoeller has apologized and yesterday, in fact, he pulled out of a tournament saying that he would not play until he can first apologize to Tiger Woods personally.

But let me weigh in with a few observations. One, there is a Bible verse that says, "Out of the abundance of the heart, the mouth speaketh." Translation, whatever is on the inside will eventually come out. I don't know if it's just plain ignorance, pompous arrogance or pure racism, but I sometimes wonder what these White men, who are otherwise accomplished and bright, are thinking when they utter these outrageous insensitivities.

Two, whether you like Tiger's insistence or not on his mixed race identity, you might as well get used to it. According to the U.S. Census, between 1960 and 1990, marriages between Blacks and Whites more than tripled. Additionally, experts believe that the rate for other groups is even higher than that, because African Americans are still less likely than other groups to marry outside of our race. Apparently, mixed race identity is the wave of the future. Get used to it.

Three, Tiger insists on calling himself a "Caublanasian" a word he made up. That is a blend of Caucasian, Black, Indian and Asian, which is what he is. But isn't it interesting that when Fuzzy Zoeller decided to dis Tiger he went straight for the fried chicken and the collard greens, not the sushi, the rice, or the noodles, but the fried chicken and the collard greens.

Four is more of a question for you to consider than it is a comment. How much time and energy should Black America really spend being frustrated and defensive about derogatory comments made in reference to specific individuals who, at best, downplay their Blackness, and, at worst, outright run away from any commitment to the African American community?

Five, with all due respect to Tiger, his talent, and his desire to be called a Caublanasian (that's his right) he and his father, at times, seem to want to straddle the fence on this Black thing. His father, Earl, was quoted before the Master's as saying that "we need a Black in a green jacket." He was, of course, referring to the green Master's jacket that the champions receive as a trophy.

Tiger, himself, doesn't seem to have a problem with Nike's marketing department when they want to market him as a Black golfer. He went on after he won, to thank Charlie Sifford and Lee Elder, Black golfers who paved the way for him to play and win the Master's. And he certainly didn't shy away at all from being compared to Jackie Robinson breaking the color barrier in baseball more than 50 years ago. Indeed, Tiger seemed to want to bask in this glory.

All I'm saying is that you have got to pick a side. Being Black is not optional and it's not seasonal. You've got to pick a side and stay on it.

Finally, what is most disturbing about this whole thing is that the press people who interviewed Fuzzy Zoeller were aware of this comment for a full week before it actually aired on *CNN*, and nobody said anything about it. Apparently Fuzzy Zoeller is not the only person who is still immune to racial sensitivity, and needs to have some racial awareness training to understand that these comments are not acceptable.

We certainly can accept Fuzzy Zoeller's apology. I do, but it doesn't make his comment right. Press people covering these kinds of nasty remarks have a duty to bring this stuff forward and not sit on it before *CNN* breaks the story a week later. For me, that is the most insulting part of this whole ordeal.

Afterthought: *I took some heat for this commentary, which I thought was rather mild. I just wanted Tiger to pick a side. Some folks thought I was too rough on the young golf phenom. Oh well!*

May 1, 1997

TJMS Topic: Race Relations: Five Years after the L.A. Riots

This week represents the fifth anniversary of the riots, the uprising, the rebellion, whatever you prefer to call what happened in Los Angeles after a White jury out in Simi Valley acquitted four White police officers of beating Black motorist, Rodney King. Almost a thousand buildings were burned to the ground, not to mention that 54 people died in that uprising and more than 2,000 folks were injured.

As the mainstream media is wondering what to do on the anniversary of such a cataclysmic event, this week everybody in the media is asking about the state of race relations in America five years later. Are they better? Are they the same? Or, are they worse? Y'all know the answer, but let me tell you this much. A poll released earlier this week found that 61%, get this, 61% of respondents in L.A. believe that another riot is likely in the next five years. Kind of makes me wonder which weekends to go back home to Los Angeles, I can tell you that.

In L.A., like most other places in America, African Americans still lag far behind White people in every leading economic indicator category. Not one, two or three but every single economic indicator category. To say nothing of the fact that, specifically in Los Angeles, the steady influx of immigrants coupled with the conservative attack on corrective programs like affirmative action have African Americans in L.A. fighting over an ever-shrinking piece of the economic pie.

Remember the Black police chief, Willie Williams, who moved to L.A. from Philadelphia to be the first Black Chief of Police in L.A.? He was forced out a couple of weeks ago. As a matter of fact that is a big story in L.A. today. They have now put an interim White police chief in his place until they figure out what to do. Meanwhile, many of the rogue cops who were identified as members of the police department in a report from the Christopher Commission are still on the L.A. police force.

I can tell you that $430 million was given to the city of L.A. by the federal government, another $310 million was kicked in by local businesses, and only $6.2 million to this day, five years later, has been allocated in terms of reinvesting in the community. You know I've got to find a way to tie this into why we ought to be involved in the process.

I remember being on the radio in L.A. the day the riots broke out. The city was burning to the ground and I was on the radio for six hours that day taking phone calls, trying to get folks to vent rather than take to the streets and burn down my neighborhood. Which didn't help, because I still lost a bunch of clothes at the cleaners and I still don't have my money back. But, on the radio that day, I took phone calls from a number of people. One brother called and was complaining about the way the jury had treated Rodney King, the fact that this verdict was nonsense, that these White folks out in Simi Valley had no business sitting on this case in the first place, and that the trial should not have been moved from downtown.

He was right about everything he said. When he took a breath, I asked him was he registered to vote. There was silence on the phone. I said, "Brother, are you still there?" He said, "Yeah, I'm here." I said, "Are you registered to vote?" He said, "No I'm not registered to vote, but what does that have to do with Rodney King getting his behind whipped by those four cops?" I said, "I will tell you. Had the trial been left in downtown Los Angeles, nobody would have called you to sit on the jury because you are not a registered voter."

To bring this full circle, we cannot be happy about the state of race relations in this country. We cannot be happy about the way the Black community is being treated, or mistreated as it were, not just in Los Angeles, but across this country. You may want to ask the question, what is it going to take for White folks to finally get it? What is it going to take for them to understand that we have a long way to go with regard to race relations and that race is still the most intractable problem in this country? At the same time, we as African Americans have to recognize that there are some things that we can do. We must be involved in the process in every way we can.

August 5, 1997

TJMS Topic: An Interview with President Clinton

Last night in my conversation with President Clinton, I tried to cover as many issues as humanly possible. In order to be reasonably successful, I had to prioritize the issues and questions that I wanted to pose. To be certain, I wanted to get to the much-talked-about apology for slavery. You might recall, when the idea first surfaced in the form of a congressional apology for slavery introduced by a White congressman from Ohio, the President appeared warm to the idea, saying, "An apology under the right circumstances, those things can be quite important." Since then having had time to gauge public interest, or disinterest as it were, the President has been rather noncommittal on the issue, as he was with me again last night.

In fairness to the President, he is not the only noncommittal individual on this issue. Indeed, many of our Black leaders are not all that excited about this idea either. Which proves once again that not all Black folks think monolithically. That is to say we don't all think the same. Which I guess is a good thing, because if we all thought like Clarence Thomas, my God, that would be ugly. And, we would all be in trouble. But on this issue, I respectfully part with some of our distinguished leaders and activists and agree with the White congressman. If we cannot do something as simple as saying we are sorry, we've got a long way to go. Of course, saying I'm sorry, excuse my English, ain't all that simple, especially in this case. Yet, we've apologized to Japanese Americans interned during World War II. We've apologized to uranium miners contaminated by nuclear tests. We've apologized to Hawaiians for the U.S. role in overthrowing the Hawaiian government over a century ago. We've apologized to victims of the Cold War radiation treatments. And, of course, we've apologized more recently to the Black men who were in the Tuskegee experiment.

But for some reason, America cannot bring herself to apologize for its most ugly and vicious display of inhumanity. Why is that? Because an apology demands an act of repentance, and that, as Big Momma would say, would be too much like right. I believe a simple apology is still the most powerful tool known to mankind. I believe it would be a first step, an important first step. Can we get on base here in dealing with the relevance of slavery in 1997? It would jump-start the national conversation that we are supposed to be having about race. It would let the healing begin. I believe it would challenge all Americans to share in the responsibility to eracism and end discrimination. President Clinton is right, an apology under the right circumstances would be important. As Dr. King said, "The time is always ripe to do right."

Afterthought: *Still no apology*

August 12, 1997

TJMS Topic: Black Man Burned and Decapitated in Elk Creek, VA

You know I hate to do this, Tom. There are some stories that you don't even want to talk about. As I often say there are no good times to be Black in America, but sometimes are worse than others. You would think that these kinds of stories would not still be happening in 1997. Last Thursday night on *BET Talk*, we were able to break a national story. Again it's not a pretty picture, but we broke this story, in part, because no one else in the national media seemed interested in putting this story out there.

An African American male by the name of Garnett Paul Johnson, who was called G.P. by his friends, lived in a little town called Elk Creek,

Virginia. This town is about an hour and a half or so outside of Roanoke, Virginia. This young man was about forty years of age, and was the person who integrated the school system in this tiny town some years ago when he was a child. As it turns out, he was out drinking and partying, apparently with two of his White friends who he had grown up with in this town of Elk Creek. At some point in the evening, they left the place where they were partying and went to one of the White males' home.

At some point in the evening, G.P., the brother, ended up being doused with gasoline, set afire and beheaded. Now, one of the White males was overheard earlier in the evening using a very common racial slur, of which we are all aware. He had been overheard using it repeatedly throughout the evening. Since his arrest, he has denied using these racial slurs and when G.P. was offered help, by another White male who has also been arrested, this man said, and I quote, "Let him smolder."

Now, as I said, this story is not being covered nationally, but the one reporter who did cover this story in this tiny town was not told by the sheriff initially that GP had been behead. From talking to family members, we also have learned that the father was never told by the sheriff initially that G.P. had been decapitated. The real kicker to this story is that the sheriff is still today saying that there is no evidence of a racially motivated hate crime. And so, because no one else is covering this story, *BET* broke it.

I promised our audience that I was going to stay on top of this, so when I finish here this morning, I'm hopping on a plane and flying to Elk Creek, Virginia. We are taking the *BET* crew with us for the show. We are going to broadcast live tonight from this tiny town and try to get some answers about what happened in Elk Creek. We learn in the news business that if it bleeds, it leads on the local news. I guess that's true as long as your blood ain't Black. You aren't hearing about this story anywhere in the national media.

I'm reminded of some of the mail that I get from time to time; the mail suggests that I concentrate on race issues too much. All I can say is, I beg to differ.

Afterthought: *The fact that we were able to break this story nationally on* BET *and talk about it further on air during the* Tom Joyner Morning Show *again underscored the importance of Black media. As I write this note, the two White male suspects await a trial for murder set to start the end of March 1998. You know I will keep you posted.*

August 14, 1997

TJMS Topic: Lessons from Elk Creek, VA

Tom, when we last talked on Tuesday morning, I was on my way to Elk Creek to help expose a tragically underexposed news story. It's kind of funny, I almost didn't make it to Elk Creek. When I went to the airport to pick up my ticket, the computer kept printing out that Tavis Smiley was traveling from Washington Dulles to Detroit. Now I love Detroit, but why they kept trying to send me to Detroit rather than Elk Creek, Virginia, I'll never know. It may be hidden racism, I don't know. But I made it to Elk Creek anyway, and I was delighted to wake up this morning and take note that here locally, at least, the *Washington Times* did a cover story on this issue. *USA Today* has a story on this today and last evening I saw *CNN* do a story about this as well. I'm happy to see that, for whatever reason, somebody is starting to pay attention to this under-reported story. That story, of course, being Garnett Paul Johnson, who was doused with gasoline, set afire and beheaded.

After traveling to Elk Creek, meeting the Johnson family, and interviewing people in the community, there is so much that I could share this morning. However, a couple of quick thoughts come to mind. One, some people took exception to the fact that I compared this horrible incident to the Jon-Benet Ramsey story on the air the other night. Now I want to clarify that. In no way do I mean, or did I mean, to devalue the life of a young child. I have long held that "three strikes" is a joke. I believe that for rape, child molestation, and murder one strike ought to be appropriate. So I think that whoever took the life of that young girl in Denver ought to be found and, quite frankly, put under the jail, with no parole. You know I personally do not support the death penalty, but murders ought to never see the light of day again.

Having said that, I believe in my heart that some stories in this country get overexposed and other stories get underexposed. I came back yesterday to the developing story, to breaking news about the Jon-Benet Ramsey autopsy report, and we're just now today getting coverage of the story of Garnett Paul Johnson. I think one has to ask why it is that one story—involving a young girl who is relatively unknown before her tragic murder—gets covered extensively, and for the other story, the national media has to be pressured and, quite frankly, pushed into giving this story any kind of coverage. That's the only comparison I intended to make. We need to be clear about the fact that when we don't cover certain stories, particularly those stories that involve African

Americans, it seems to me that the media does a disservice by putting forward the image, at least, that we do not value Black life. I believe that all humanity is worth something. That is why I was so outraged, the folks at *BET* were outraged, and I know you were as well, that this story was not being covered.

Additionally, we need to be just as outraged about Black on Black crime as we are when horrendous stories like this one in Elk Creek, Virginia, surface as well. The bottom line is that all of us—including the press and the Black community—need to start valuing all of humanity.

August 19, 1997

TJMS Topic: Abner Louima: The Good, the Bad and the Ugly

Abner Louima is a thirty-year-old Haitian immigrant who was alledgelly beaten and sodomized by the New York Police Department (NYPD). Somehow, even though he worked as a security guard and was trying to break up a fight, he ended up being arrested himself by New York's "finest." The story didn't stop there. They took him back to the precinct where they beat him, took a toilet plunger and rammed it up his rectum, then threw him in a cell. They left him bleeding for some ninety minutes before anyone came in to check on him and finally called paramedics to come help him.

He has now sued the city for an outrageous amount of money. Well, I shouldn't say outrageous. He is absolutely on point. He ought to get as much as he can. Now, I think there are four things worth taking note of about this case. One, credit must be given to Mayor Giuliani, a Republican, whom I've never supported, but in this particular case, he did the right thing. He and the police chief, within forty-eight hours of this occurring arrested the first two cops and, as you know, two more were arrested yesterday. They suspended the supervising sergeant in charge without pay, removed the entire precinct command structure, and appealed to the NYPD to breakdown the so-called "blue wall of silence," which led to the arrest of the second officer. One of the officers on the force actually came forward and turned in the second cop. All this was accomplished within forty-eight hours.

Two, this is terribly significant because what typically happens when something like this goes down is the police force, the mayor, and everybody else in town tries to double-talk their way out of the issue. They try to defend the officers' intentions, saying they were provoked. They try not to offend the police officers' union. They refuse to fully cooperate with the investigating authorities. It seems, at first glance that in this case, none of those things happened in New York, to the credit of Mayor Giuliani.

But three, what is troublesome about this is that the cops and the police chief, who we happened to have on the show last night, still refuse to call this incident a racist incident. It reminds me of what we talked about a week or so ago—Garnett Paul Johnson, down in Virginia. You got a guy who is doused, set afire, beheaded and the local sheriff still won't say the crime was racially motivated. I don't know when we are going to get to the point when you see nonsense like this go down, where race is written all over it, that the folks in charge will step forth with courage and say this was racist, it was wrong, and it won't be defended.

Finally, even when White folks do the right thing, as the police chief and mayor did in this case, for some reason they find it almost impossible to come forth and talk to the Black media about it. Now again, to the credit of the police chief, he came on last night. But you would not believe and I ain't got time to tell you, excuse my English, the pulling, the prodding, the begging, the pleading, and the threatening I had to do to get the police chief to come on last night and talk to us about this on Black Entertainment Television. At some point, we've got to get to the place where this kind of madness stops. But when it does happen, those folks in charge need to quit running away from addressing the Black folks who are victimized by the nonsense of folks who they supervise.

Being from L.A. is why I'm extra sensitive to this issue. I know how this would have gone down had it happened in L.A. some years ago. Now in L.A. we have, our second new police chief in five years. He happens to be an African American. Bernard Parks, the new chief out in L.A., is a good guy. But under Daryl Gates's tenure, when something like this went down, like the Rodney King case, there was shucking and jiving, blaming somebody else, trying to beat around the bush, and defending the officers. Mayor Giuliani in this particular incident deserves credit for how he handled the situation. But far too often, across the country, folks in Chicago, Philadelphia and Miami know that's not usually the way it goes down.

Afterthought: *We'll see what happens with the Louima case now that the Dream Team of Johnnie L. Cochran, Jr., Barry Scheck and Peter Neufeld are Louima's lead attorneys.*

September 30, 1997

TJMS Topic: The Little Rock Nine

Following the big show in Little Rock on Friday, I eventually made it back here in Washington to appear as I regularly do on *CNN's Capital Gang Sunday.* Being that the show always has three segments to it, we were discussing campaign finance reform in one segment, the IRS scandal last week in another segment, and in the final segment, we were going to discuss integration following the celebration of the Little Rock Nine last week. One of my colleagues, who I actually like a lot, very nice guy, during one of the commercial breaks, suggested that we cut the conversation on integration and spend more time discussing the other topics because "the people don't want to talk about integration."

And so I looked up during the commercial break, and the people must have read my eyes because it got so quiet that you could hear a pin drop, and I asked him, what people he was talking about? What people don't want to discuss integration and for that matter, what kind of scientific survey did you take to tell you what the people want to talk about? It reminds me of the O.J. case. I just got tired of hearing people say the American people haven't bought the verdict in the O.J. Simpson case. What American people are you talking about? Are we not American people? Those persons who, Black and White, happen to agree with the verdict in that case—are we not Americans?

I mean, to be sure, Black folks weren't jumping up and down volunteering to be Black when God was handing out colors. Certainly not Whoopi Goldberg. We're Black and we are proud to be

Americans, but we certainly did not ask for this harassment that we often get as Black folks. Sometimes, too often, quite frankly, we are accused of being obsessed with race. We get told all the time, get over it. We talked about this last night on the television program. "Get over it, my granddad didn't own any slaves." Well, maybe he didn't, but you certainly—whether you like it or not—have been the recipient, the beneficiary oftentimes, of what Senator Bill Bradley once called "White skin privilege."

I would much rather come on everyday and listen to J. and George talk about each other's Momma, but the point is that we are forced to discuss issues of racism because they arise. And so it's against this backdrop that the President's race relations commission meets again in Washington with a number of provocative and, quite frankly, explosive issues which face them. Mainly the issue of whether or not the commission's work ought to focus in on the issue of multiculturalism as opposed to this Black and White divide.

Dr. John Hope Franklin, the chairman, says the commission's work ought to focus on the Black/White divide. Angela Oh, a Korean commissioner, says that the commission's work ought to focus on multiculturalism. So the President is challenged to provide some leadership on how we are going to attack this most divisive issue in the country. The issue of whether or not he is going to offer an apology for slavery is back on the table again today. The issue of reparations remains on the table. But whatever the President decides to do, we've got to move from talking just about symbolism to talking about substance.

We as Black folks understand that what the Little Rock Nine went through, what we celebrated last week, what those in the Civil Rights Movement went through, was about access. It wasn't about being able to sit next to some White kid in a classroom, or drink out of the same water fountain, or use the same washroom. It was about access, and without access there can be no success. You've got to have access to education, access to employment, access to capital. We've all been blessed with some talent, but talent without the opportunity, the talent without the access, doesn't yield you anything. At the end of this conversation, we've got to talk about access. Access to education, access to employment and access to capital, and if we don't bring the conversation full circle to discuss those issues, then quite frankly this commission really is a joke. I never did tell you whether or not we discussed integration on the show after the break. We did. We discussed it and we were successful in making sure that we didn't cut the time allotted. As far as I was concerned, and I enjoy doing *CNN*, it was actually the most interesting, the most spirited part of the show. But it just goes to show you that oftentimes people, without even knowing it, say things that do not take into consideration the feelings, concerns and issues of other people. They are so quick to say, "the American people" and somehow we oftentimes just get left out of that group conveniently.

October 7, 1997

TJMS Topic: From Slavery to Freedom

Tom, you know every now and then in life you find yourself caught up in a particular golden moment. One that you know will become lasting and special. I think we've all been fortunate to have had a few. I certainly have. Accompanying Dr. Maya Angelou on my very first trip to Africa, once doing a joint book signing with Rosa Parks, having the chance to chat with Nelson Mandela, visiting the El Mina Slave Castles in Ghana with the great Black historian, Dr. John Henrik Clarke. And then, last Friday night, attending a private and intimate dinner in Chicago with noted Black historian, Dr. John Hope Franklin.

Now of late, we all have come to know more about Professor John Hope Franklin, thanks to President Clinton appointing him as the Chair of his Race Commission. What you may not know is that this year we celebrate the fiftieth anniversary of Dr. Franklin's acclaimed book, *From Slavery to Freedom*, which is arguably the most authoritative history of African Americans. First published in 1947 and now in its seventh edition, *From Slavery to Freedom* ought to be required reading for all Black Americans, and for that matter, White Americans as well. As I sat a few feet away from Dr. Franklin last Friday evening, I wished that every one of our loyal listeners could have been in that room with me listening to one of our master teachers talk about our vast human odyssey of more than one thousand years and the continuing struggle for equality in America.

Because the meeting was private and off-the-record, I'm prohibited from sharing anything that was said in the meeting that would violate that trust. But as I sat mesmerized by Dr. Franklin, so powerful and prolific, more than a few thoughts crossed my mind.

One, as part of this national conversation on race that the President wants us to have, we need to figure out a way to help educate White America on our struggle and our contributions. I don't know, maybe having Oprah select Dr. Franklin's book is a good place to start. But I'm convinced that much of racism is based to this day on ignorance.

Two, young Black professionals, the beneficiaries of this struggle, need to check ourselves. Too many of us are slaves to our careers and are never of service to our communities.

Three, Black folks need to wed themselves to proven programs and not necessarily prolific leaders. When one leader retires, dies, betrays us or just moves on, we need to keep on moving. Programs, not people.

Four, America may be desegregated, but is it truly integrated? Two entirely different things, you know.

And finally, it is not just the past issue of slavery that must be confronted, but to be more frank, the present, the uncomfortable issue of White supremacy. The very notion that the color of one's skin makes one superior. None of us are slaves today, but at one point or another, we all confront somebody who disses us just because we are Black and they are not. Police brutality, housing discrimination, being passed over for promotion, loan denial, it ain't cute and God ain't in it. The notion that White is better than Black is making a comeback. There's *The Bell Curve, The End of Racism*, books full of racist jargon written by White academics and somehow passed off as scholarship. A waste of good trees, if you ask me.

We cannot move forward on race relations in America, unless and until the most uncomfortable issue of White superiority and White supremacy is challenged. And I don't know if we are ready to go there just yet in America.

I wish everybody could have been there. As this debate about race moves forward in this country, I hope that we will all get a chance to hear more from Dr. Franklin, just a thought.

Afterthought: *Another commentary that on air, could not come close to expressing how I felt that night sitting at the feet of a great American, Dr.*

John Hope Franklin. This commentary represented the first, and only, time I've ever uttered the phrase "white supremacy" on air. I find that the term, although real, unnerves some folks. Only a moderate number of hate calls followed this commentary—no bomb threats today.

December 16, 1997

TJMS Topic: The Moral Majority

Tom, how many times have you heard the statistic that one out of every three Black men is in prison, on parole or on probation? One out of every three Black men is caught up somehow in the criminal justice system. I heard it again just the other day on Black talk radio. I'm always reminding Black folks that if one out of every three of us is on lockdown or somehow entangled with the law, then that means that two out of every three of us, the majority, for those who didn't major in math, the majority of us, are trying to do the right thing everyday. Fundamentally, it always amazes me that we are so quick and carefree to recite and, quite frankly, translate statistics that are not necessarily negative into negative damning declarations about ourselves.

I'm not suggesting at all that criminal behavior in the Black community ought to go unchecked or be tolerated, quite the opposite. I recognize, as do you, that Black folks are the disproportionate victims of violent crimes. We're the ones who are being innocently killed in drive-bys. We're the ones being assaulted and raped. We're the ones being robbed at gunpoint. It's our children that the crack dealers are targeting and recruiting as runners and lookouts, giving a whole new meaning to the term neighborhood watch. If anybody wants crime under control, I suspect it's us.

I also recognize though that when a Black kills a White, he gets the death penalty. When a White kills a Black, we want to take to the streets and start rioting. But when a Black kills another Black, we act as if nothing happened. Nobody heard, nobody saw, nobody knows anything, and yet everybody knows where Neck Bone and Dante live. I guess we think by closing our eyes and plugging our ears, we can ignore and avoid the crime that has crept, rather walked upright and boldly into our neighborhoods. We apparently don't realize that silence only serves to embolden those who are destroying our beloved community.

And so for us, crime is real, not a rhetorical issue. Consequently we need to make sure that we continue taking proactive steps to turn the tide against crime. I guess in the final analysis my point is a simple one. I just don't think we can get there from here. That is to say, I think many of us are to psychologically damaged, even we are starting to believe that most Black men are or will become property of the penal system. Not me and not most of the brothers who I know. Yet, those who commit crimes in our community are no different than those who commit crimes in other communities.

The truth is most Whites are killed by other Whites. But as my friend always tells me, you never hear the term White-on-White crime. And in any community, there is always a small cadre of fools who just won't do right. But again, THEY are in the minority. WE, the law-abiding, hardworking, volunteering, taxpaying, education-getting, career-building, family-loving, God-fearing Black folks are in the majority. We are in the majority. It is a simple enough point to make, perhaps too simple for some, but I tell you that we aren't about to wave a white flag. Evil only triumphs when good men and women do nothing.

AND ANOTHER THING...

December 10, 1996

Tom Joyner Morning Show Topic: Top Ten Things I Hate about the O.J. Saga

Today I want to give my top ten list of the things I hate most about the O.J. Simpson saga.

Number ten, I hate when people say that no intelligent, thinking, rational individual with good sense could deem O.J. Simpson not guilty. In other words, if we don't agree with their opinion, then we are suddenly unintelligent, non-thinking, irrational individuals with no good sense. I hate that.

Number nine, I hate when pundits repeatedly say that O.J. Simpson has been found guilty in the court of public opinion, that America is outraged by the verdict. Now stay with me on this one. If all the polls, studies and surveys indicate that O.J. Simpson was deemed not guilty by most Black Americans, that means that Johnnie L. Cochran did a good job of proving reasonable doubt. So either Black folks are not Americans or what the pundits really mean to say is that White Americans were outraged by the verdict. But don't try to play us like we ain't Americans.

Number eight, I hate that the civil trial is not being televised because we are forced to rely on the media spin about what's going on inside the court-room rather than being allowed to make our own assessments.

Number seven, I hate that a man who was acquitted by a jury of his peers is fighting a civil trial and at the same time fighting in another courtroom to get his children back. No matter what you think of O.J. Simpson, guilty or innocent, the man was found not guilty by a jury of his peers. What has he done to not entitle him to custody of his two kids? Only as a

Black man in America could you be found not guilty and then find yourself in another courtroom fighting to get your children back.

Number six, I hate that the critics all of a sudden act like they care about Sidney and Justin, and that that's their primary concern—the children's welfare. How can you be concerned about their welfare when you are cutting this man off at the knees and denying him any opportunity to make an income? Who is going to take care of the children? You can't act like you care about the children, and then deny the man an opportunity to earn any kind of income.

Number five, I hate that some people declare definitively that O.J. Simpson got away with murder, as if they were in the bushes that night on Bundy. Apparently, there were a whole bunch of eyewitnesses who didn't come forth and testify at the trial.

Number four, I hate that folks raise hell about the first jury being basically all Black, and then they've got nothing to say about the second jury being overwhelmingly White. Race is not an issue in the case of the second jury.

Number three, I hate that people cannot distinguish between one's strong defense of what he or she believes to be right, and one embracing O.J. Simpson. Like most Black Americans, I'm not a friend or a fan of O.J. Simpson, but I do believe, as my Big Momma always says, that right is right, and don't wrong anybody. And I think you can talk about what you deem to be right, and at the same time, not be in bed with O.J. Simpson. But people can't distinguish between taking that position and loving O.J. Simpson.

Number two, I hate that I can sit on a television show, the *Charles Grodin* show, and have a White man on the show, live on television, say that O.J. Simpson ought to hang himself. That he ought to kill himself and take himself out of America's misery.

I mean if I had said that about any White American, that he ought to just kill himself, I would be summarily dismissed from every talk show on television. But a White man can sit around on a show with me and say O.J. ought to kill himself, and nobody raises any hell about it. I don't quite understand that.

Finally, number one, I hate, really hate that I had to spend my time talking about what I hate about the O.J. Simpson trial.

Afterthought: *More Juice*?

January 23, 1997

TJMS Topic: Has the Jury Reached a Verdict?

You know Tom, I was noting this morning that over the past two weeks, a number of incidents have really knocked this O.J. Simpson story off of the front pages. We've had the Jon-Benet Ramsey story, the young girl who was killed, the unfortunate, untimely and tragic death of Ennis Cosby, Bill Cosby's only son, and the inauguration of the President. A number of stories have knocked the O.J. Simpson story off the front pages including the bombing of the Planned Parenthood building in Atlanta. But it is now back with a vengeance because we are now in the closing argument phase. Thank God it's not the opening argument phase.

Let me make a prediction. I think O.J. Simpson's chances of being found not liable in this trial are slim to none, and Slim is out of town. There are three reasons I think he's going to lose this case:

One, there is a lower burden of proof, just the

preponderance of the evidence or in other words, the jury only has to believe that there's a 51% chance that he more than likely committed the murders. This lowers it much less than the first trial, so I think that with the lower burden of proof, he's going to lose.

Two, this case, despite what everybody wants to say, is a race case and has been from the very beginning. And we have a White jury in this case, who will have to go back to their White neighborhoods and explain—in the face of all the evidence and in light of what the first jury did—how they let this man off a second time. How do you explain this to your White neighbors? I don't know how they're going to go back home to Santa Monica and do that. The Black folks didn't have to come back to South Central or any place else they lived and explain to their Black neighbors how they let him go. The White folks have a different situation.

Three, I feel the media really screwed up, given the way they maligned this first jury calling them stupid and ignorant. How could they have done this? I mean, they were called everything but the children of God by the media. I think because the White jury saw how the first jury was treated, they are not going to set themselves up to be maligned and demonized the way the first jury was in the criminal trial.

Finally, when all is said and done, it really doesn't matter what happens, because you know as well I do that if he's found liable he's going to appeal. God knows he has grounds, and fertile grounds on which to appeal. And if he's found not liable, then you know all heck is going to break loose. There is no way in this great country called America that a Black man is supposed to go through the criminal justice system and come out 3 and 0, even if he is O.J. Simpson. Winning the criminal case, getting his kids back, and winning the civil trial? The media and

White America are not going to let that go. Please.

Afterthought: *Hate to say I told you so...so I won't.*

February 6, 1997

TJMS Topic: Verdict: Liable

Let me give you my top ten observations after the verdict.

One, I told you a while ago that his chances of winning were slim to none and Slim was out of town.

Two, White folks still don't get it. I saw a number of commentators asking, as the verdict was about to be read, whether or not Black folks were going to riot in the streets of Los Angeles. As if somehow our hopes and dreams and aspirations were wrapped around O.J. Simpson, and for some reason, whatever happened, we were going to go in the streets and burn down the city. I don't think so.

Three, did you notice that there weren't any cameras parked in locations where White folks were jumping up and down like the Howard students were? You didn't see any cameras parked out in places where White folks hang to see if they were going to be jumping up and down. And you know White folks were celebrating, but they didn't park those cameras in those strategic places and didn't show us that a thousand and one times day in and day out.

Four, why is it wrong for Black folks to celebrate anyway? Why can't we celebrate? If you wanted to celebrate, if you thought O.J. Simpson was innocent, why couldn't you celebrate at the end of the first trial? White folks want to tell you when to be born, when to die, when to laugh, when to cry, and when to jump up and down. That's not right.

Five, why does everyone want to say that now the healing should begin? Isn't that Rodney King's line, "Can't we all just get along?" That's plagiarism at best, trying to take Rodney King's line. Everybody wants the healing to begin, now that they've gotten what they wanted.

Six, you know everybody is dogging O.J. for having a party. Can't a brother have a party? How are they going to dictate to O.J. whether he can have a party in his own house?

Seven, if you notice, everybody is now calling the verdict in this civil trial a common sense verdict. That the jury did the right thing. What does that say about the first jury? They had no common sense? They did the wrong thing? It's a terrible analogy.

Eight, the judgment in this case for compensatory damages of $8.5 million, is way out of line given California precedents. You're talking in the range of $100,000 for a grown son who has been murdered. $8.5 million is way out of line by any California standard, for a White person or a Black person. And the punitive damages are obviously going to go much higher.

Nine, I take nothing away from the families. If I were a member of the Brown or the Goldman family and I thought this guy or anybody else had gotten away with the murder of my son or my daughter, I would have gone to a civil trial as well. So they are right to do what they want to do. However, I'm sick and tired of all the praise that's being heaped upon Daniel Petrocelli, as if he's the greatest thing since sliced bread.

Johnnie L. Cochran won a case against all the odds and, quite frankly, against a lot of the evidence. And nobody wanted to give Johnnie his props. The mainstream media vilified Johnnie L. Cochran. And now there is a movement to get him off of his *Court TV* show. That's not right.

Finally, for the families...this Simpson saga, clearly, was about getting justice as they saw it. Justice is a very abstract concept. Justice is what each of us determines it to be. So I understand their point of view. But I'm tired of hearing folks now try to say this is not about race. It always was, it is now, and forever shall be in the annals of history a case about race. Can I get a witness?

Afterthought: *Okay, I can't resist. I told you so!*

April 17, 1997

TJMS Topic: The Chittlin' Circuit

In a recent issue of *Time* magazine, the cover story profiled the 25 most influential people in America for 1997 as selected by the editors at the magazine. As *Time* magazine puts it "powerful people twist your arms, influentials just sway your way of thinking." Last year, African Americans Oprah Winfrey, Minister Louis Farrakhan, Harvard Professor William Julius Wilson, and Wynton Marsalis were on the list. By the way, congratulations to the incomparable Wynton Marsalis, jazz musician and composer, who was recently awarded the first ever Pulitzer Prize for a jazz-based composition. Way to go Wynton!

Time magazine's class of 1997 includes a few Black folks, specifically Tiger Woods, Colin Powell, Kenneth "Babyface" Edmonds, and the Chairman of Harvard's Afro-American Studies Department, Henry Louis "Skip" Gates, Jr. And speaking of Skip Gates and his influence, I read a piece by Gates recently which indeed influenced my thinking.

In the piece, Gates raises a question about the so-called chittlin' circuit. The chittlin' circuit is about to get back into full swing now that summer is in fact approaching. The chittlin' circuit is the popular Black theater on tour which often features out-of-work Black television actors, comics and musicians. Now we all know these plays well, so I won't labor rambling off their names. But according to Skip Gates, the king of the hill on the chittlin' circuit is a man named Shelley Garrett. He reportedly earned, get this, $15 to $25 million for one play—a play that grossed an estimated $600,000 a week in the city of Atlanta alone! Clearly these plays make a lot of money.

Very quickly, let me quote from Gates in this article which appeared in *The New Yorker* magazine, "The fact that the audience at the Sarah Vaughn Concert Hall is entirely Black creates an essential dynamic. I mentioned elements of comic relief. They include a Black preacher greedy for grandma's chicken wings, a randy old man trailing toilet paper from a split seam in the back of his pants, the grandmother herself, whose churchiness is outlandishly caricatured, and endless references to a particular character's lapses of personal hygiene. All the very worst stereotypes of the race are on display larger than life. Here in this racially sequestered space, a Black audience laughs uninhibitedly. Whereas the presence of White folks would have engendered a familiar anxiety. Will they think that's what we're really like? If this drama were shown on television or in any integrated forum, Jesse Jackson would probably denounce it, the NAACP would demand a boycott, and every soul in the theater would swap his or her finery for sandwich boards in order to picket it. You don't want White people to see this kind of spectacle."

The question which Gates raises is how Black

America would respond if the chittlin' circuit were produced and/or consumed by White America. A most legitimate question. One, quite frankly, that I don't have the time to delve into this morning with regard to my personal viewpoint. That's really not the point of my offering this morning anyway, although you know I have an opinion. But again as *Time* puts it, influentials sway our way of thinking, and Gates, as usual, gives us something to think about this summer while we are waiting in line on the chittlin' circuit.

Afterthought: *I'm not big on the chittlin' circuit, but I love chittlins'!*

May 15, 1997

TJMS Topic: Support Black Businesses!

Black Enterprise magazine just released its twenty-fifth annual listing of the top 100 Black-owned industrial and service firms in the country. In short, what *Black Enterprise* reports is that while sales at Black-owned companies rose 7.75% over the past year, the pace of growth for the nation's top Black-owned businesses slowed considerably over the past year. Translation, some Black businesses made a whole lot of money over the last year but far too many Black businesses never really had a chance to get off the ground. Those that are up and running did not have an opportunity to expand their growth rate.

The magazine suggests that much of the hostile business environment that Black businesses must operate in is due to the all-out-attack on affirmative action and minority set-aside programs. Indeed, just last week the Clinton administration announced new proposals to further curb minority set-aside programs or some $200 million in federal contracts. Now let me briefly remind us of three things we need to reconsider, especially at a time when disturbing news about the slowed rate of Black business growth hits us in the face, as it does in this *Black Enterprise* article.

One, government indifference leads to corporate indifference. When the government doesn't care about assisting Black businesses you can bet your last dollar that corporate America will also look the other way, head for the hills and run for cover, despite the purchasing power of Black America.

Two, and make no mistake about this, the attack on affirmative action does in fact trickle down. It's real simple. A loss of profit equals a loss of jobs.

When profits are up, you can hire more people. For example, the company that I work for, BET Holdings, was *Black Enterprise* magazine's "Black business of the year." According to the magazine, profits for BET Holdings rose some 20%. They expanded, opened up a restaurant, and have addtional new ventures. BET Holdings hired more people over the last year because they were able to expand. It's real simple.

When you attack Black business, you are essentially attacking Black people. Folks always make the argument that affirmative action only benefits the rich in the Black community. That's nonsense. Who do you think these Black folks hire? They hire Black people. When these minority set-aside programs are wiped out, they can't hire as many people. Ultimately, rich Black folks are going to be okay. Bob Johnson is doing quite well. Earl Graves and John Johnson are doing well. But the folks who are most likely to get hurt when Black businesses are under attack are those of us with jobs at Black businesses.

Finally, more than ever this report from *Black Enterprise* underscores the real reason we all need to support Black businesses every single opportunity that we get. We talk a good game, but not enough of us support Black businesses in the way that we ought to support them. I hope the message that comes through is that now, more than ever, we need to do everything we can to support those brothers and sisters who are trying on a daily basis to keep Black businesses afloat in our community.

Afterthought: *I hope you bought this book at a Black-owned book store!*

May 29, 1997

TJMS Topic: Nike and the Black Community or Nike in the Black Community?

Yesterday Tom, while sitting courtside in the gym lacing my sneakers and preparing to get my game on, I began to check out the assortment of shoes adorning the feet of the brothers on the court. I wasn't really surprised to discover that Nike was the shoe of choice, as you might suspect. But I was somewhat shocked to note that only two brothers in the gym were not wearing Nike sneakers. My informal survey would seem a simple mundane reality to most people, but you know me. No observation is merely a simple mundane reality. Such realities are the stuff that commentaries are made of, so here goes....

Let me say to Phil Knight, Nike's brilliant founder and visionary, I ain't mad at you. In fact, full disclosure would have me tell you that I was lacing up a pair of Nike's yesterday too. Nike, in the truest sense of capitalism, has crushed the competition in their ads and artwork as far as I'm concerned. Have you seen the latest Michael Jordan commercial, "That's why I succeed"? That commercial is all that and a bag of onion potato chips with the funk on them! More power to Michael Jordan, Tiger Woods and every other professional athlete who is getting paid for just doing it.

Now having said that, I've got a quick suggestion for Mr. Knight and his creative crew at Nike. The city of Detroit is bouncing back economically in a major way. Give it up to Detroit's Mayor Dennis Archer who is leading the way to bring business back into the Motor City by having a significant part of the city declared a federal, state and local enterprise zone. Which basically means that if big business sets up shop within the boundaries of the enterprise zone, they get rewarded with federal, state and local tax credits based on the folks that they hire. In other words, when you're in the zone, you can leave the taxes alone.

Not to mention that the department of Housing and Urban Development, the sponsoring governmental agency, is just itching to offer technical assistance to those who qualify and take advantage of what is essentially a tax-free opportunity. And it's working. The Motor City is revving up once again, and the state of Michigan, for the first time, has replaced the state of New York as the leader in the *Black Enterprise* Top 100 businesses survey. Twenty-four of the top 100 Black-owned businesses are now located in the state of Michigan. Now, back to my suggestion. Is there a better place in America for Nike to build a shoe plant than Detroit, Michigan?

Tax credits, folks who need jobs, a city making a comeback. A bold move by Nike could help turn a whole city around. No, it's not as cheap as building a factory in Indonesia, but folks in Indonesia, excuse my English, ain't wearing $150 and $185 shoes either.

The next time you see my favorite college coach, John Thompson, from Georgetown, who was on Nike's board, or former Atlanta Mayor Andrew Young, who I understand is now a paid consultant to Nike on international relations, you might want to pass on this suggestion. I might add that both of these are great Black men. But tell them, when you see them, that you don't want the children in Indonesia exploited by Nike, but you don't want the kids in Cleveland, Philly or Detroit exploited either.

Afterthought: *Just in case you were curious, there's still no Nike plant in urban America.*

July 1, 1997

TJMS Topic: Tyson Embarrassed Who...?

Tom, this Tyson incident gives rise to a thousand topics, not to mention jokes. I know what happened in Las Vegas Saturday night is a comic's dream. I think I've heard enough jokes and enough commentary, but make room for one more.

If the incident weren't ugly enough, there is a particular comment that I've heard more than a few times since Saturday night, including live on our show last evening. And I've got to tell you this morning that I'm starting to feel like Popeye—"I've stood all I can stands, and I can't stands no more." So let me comment on this. How many times since Saturday night have you heard someone say, "Mike Tyson embarrassed us?" "You know the White folks already think we act like animals, and that's exactly what he acted like, an animal. He embarrassed us." Excuse me? Embarrassed us? I don't think so.

Mike Tyson embarrassed himself. If I'm embarrassed at all, I'm embarrassed for him. I'm embarrassed for his co-manager, who acted like a fool, talking about Evander Holyfield live on television. I'm even embarrassed for Evander Holyfield's trainer. When asked whether or not he'd ever seen anything like this, the trainer said, "Yes, in Harlem." Man, how are you going to dis Harlem like that?

Mike Tyson is not a representative of any of us. We ought to quit that nonsense telling folks that Mike Tyson embarrassed us. I don't think that White folks are going to quit comparing all of us just because I'm upset about it. Somebody once said that we all ought to be judged by the best we can produce in our race, and not by the worst. I'm not at all suggesting that they are going to stop comparing all of us, but I do believe that we have to stop buying into this mindset of thinking that because one of us acts a fool, that we are all fools. That's absolutely nonsense.

What matters most is that we all have a healthy sense of self-respect, self-determination and self-assurance. That's what Evander Holyfield had, and that's in part, I think, why he beat Mike Tyson. Mike Tyson is not a reflection on any of us and we ought to quit buying into that mindset. You don't know Mike, and Mike doesn't know you. The misdeeds of one brother are not applicable to all the rest of us Black men.

A lot of young folks are trying to explain, trying to rationalize away what Mike did. I think that's somewhat indicative of the generation gap in our country, certainly in our community. I say it's indicative because that's the world in which they live. Oftentimes you see young African American men, unfortunately too often, having to resort to that kind of violence, that kind of retaliation. You know, that "I'm going to get mine" mentality, that mentality of individualism. But now that Mike has apologized, I don't know where that leaves those people.

Afterthought: *Sometimes I feel like I'm rambling in my commentaries—like today. But Mike Tyson didn't embarrass me—he played himself!*

July 15, 1997

TJMS Topic: Is Reverend Lyons Lying?

Good morning, Tom. Yesterday, as you know, was a travel day for me and so I didn't get a chance to hear the show. But I know you all must have clowned the Reverend Henry Lyons of the National Baptist Convention U.S.A.. I know you did. I'm tempted to crack a few jokes myself. But there is at the heart of this matter an issue or two that I think needs to be addressed in earnest and then we can get back to the jokes.

Let me commence with a brief word for all the upstanding, righteous, godly, ethical and moral men of the cloth. I feel your pain. Don't you just hate it when a member of your chosen profession, a prominent member, no less, apparently engages in acts that only serve to reinforce every ugly thing that people already believe about your work and service? For those who may not know (and I don't understand how you don't), the Reverend Dr. Henry Lyons, head of the 8.5 million member National Baptist Convention U.S.A., saw his wife arrested last week on arson charges for starting a fire at a posh waterfront home he owns with another woman. At the moment, Dr. Lyons is being thoroughly questioned about his alleged infidelity and dubious finances. In addition to a waterfront home, this picture also includes a brand new Mercedes, a brand new Rolls Royce and a 20-carat diamond ring.

Well, as you might suspect, as soon as Dr. Lyons could get back into the pulpit, he started preaching that "Daniel in the lion's den" sermon. You know the one... "Well, I've been persecuted and prosecuted, demonized and destroyed, sensationalized and scandalized, bastardized and betrayed, punished and penalized by a White-owned media." Only time will tell whether Dr. Lyons is lying. But I can tell you right now, Dr. Lyons is tripping. I think I have figured out why God made both Black and White. Each one of us needs somebody to blame when we act a fool and get caught up in some mess.

This is not about Black and White, it's about wrong and right. Isn't it amazing how preachers are always telling us to call on God when we get into trouble, but when trouble rises in their lives, they hasten not to the throne, but to the abuse excuse, the blame game—"the White man is out to get me." The bottom line is that you can't preach virtue unless you are virtuous. The problem is when Black leaders blame all of their misdeeds, or in this case, their alleged infidelity and funny money practices on racism, it makes a mockery of real incidents of racism. And as we all know, there are still far too many of those.

Yesterday President Clinton's advisory committee on race relations met for the first time in the White House. At a time when we ought to be taking racism seriously, this kind of blame game by the Reverend Lyons, with all due respect, is essentially a joke. Tonight on *BET Talk*, we are going to spend the entire show, no guests, taking people's phone calls about this incident and what they think of the Black church and its ministers. Again, I don't want to take a broad brush and paint all Black ministers with the same color paint, as I said in the opening. We want to give Black America a chance tonight on *BET Talk* to talk about this and to see what they think of this whole incident, and of what Dr. Lyons is saying with regard to blaming his misfortune on the White man. Now Tom, get back to the jokes.

Afterthought: *Dr. Lyons did come on my* BET *program and it was quite a lively discussion. The Reverend Lyons appeared humble and contrite. His lawyer attempted to answer all the questions and the viewer phone calls were mostly challenging and confrontational, to my surprise. He has since been charged with racketeering and embezzlement by the federal government and is awaiting trial as I write this notation.*

October 14, 1997

TJMS Topic: What's in a Name?

Let me talk briefly this morning about hyphenated-Americans. First of all, I don't even spell African American with a hyphen. People like Whoopi Goldberg and others, act as if dropping the term African off of African American can somehow end discrimination and racism. All of a sudden we will be accepted as equals in the American system. I say it didn't happen when we were Negroes, it didn't happen when we were Colored, and it sure didn't happen when we were Black. I actually remember that last period.

I don't think dropping the term African off African American ensures that we are somehow going to be treated as equals. Before the term came up, we were living in a country that was separate and unequal, and this is not going to change just because we drop the term African.

It is possible, believe it or not, to have both pride and patriotism, to be proud of your African descent, and at the same time to be proud to be an American. The two are not mutually exclusive. I've had the opportunity to travel to a few places around the world, not unlike a lot of folks, and I'm happy to go abroad, but I'm always happier to come back home. Of all the places that I've been, despite all the problems we have here in America, I'd still rather live here. This is just Tavis talking. I'd still rather be living here than anyplace else. You know, I'm happy to go, but I'm happy to come home.

I'm proud to be of African descent and proud to be an American. One does not mean you've got to give up the other. It is not anti-American to call yourself an African American. It almost reminds me of this debate on affirmative action that we continue to have. You've always got folks saying, "Well, we shouldn't trade quality for diversity. Why pass over top talent for racial preference?" Excuse me? Sometimes the most qualified person for the job is the African American candidate. It is possible, you know, in 1997, to be both Black and qualified. It's not an either or situation.

Dr. Maya Angelou in her brilliant poem, "On the Pulse of Morning," which she read during the first inauguration of Bill Clinton, said "we were bought, stolen and sold into slavery, arriving on a nightmare, praying for a dream." Now I've always maintained that the various name changes that we've endured down through the years really represent a search for a lost cultural identity, stolen cultural identity. We were searching for a name that would reflect our history. A name that would reflect our origin. Negro, Black, Colored didn't exactly do that.

Nobody seems too bothered by the Irish Americans in Boston or the Italian Americans in New York, or even the Native Americans, but somehow this term African American seems to get people all bent out of shape and brings out cries of anti-American behavior. No, what's anti-American is denying a people's right to self-realization and self-determination. In other words, I don't really care what you call yourself, just don't call me late for dinner and it doesn't really matter to me. But it is rather interesting that nobody Black who I know gives even a passing thought to how White Americans, excuse me, White people, I shouldn't use that hyphenated term, how White people choose to identify themselves. As my Big Momma always said, there are twenty-four hours in the day. Twelve hours to mind your business, and twelve hours to leave other folks's business alone.

It's kind of hard when you live in a color-conscious and color-coded society to not be identified by color or race, even if, like Whoopi, you abhor the title. Every poll, study, and survey in America always divides us by race, including the census. Shakespeare said, "What's in a name? A rose by any other name would still smell just as sweet." Smiley said, "What's in a name? By any other name, Black folks still lag far behind White Americans in every single leading economic indicator category."

Some things are deeper than a name change, if you know what I mean. Some things that aren't going to change without a change. On a certain level, it almost doesn't matter what you call yourself anyway. As I've said before, you know when they get ready to dis you, they know exactly where to go. When Fuzzy Zoeller decided to dis Tiger Woods, Mr. Caublanasian, he went right for the fried chicken and the collard greens, not the sushi and rice. In the final analysis, if we spent less time talking about what to call one another, and more time talking about how to treat one another, don't you think we'd be a lot better off?

September 23, 1997

TJMS Topic: Black Conservatives: Oxymoron or Alternative?

Tom, we all remember in 1995 and early 1996 when General Colin Powell kept would-be opponents biting their fingernails and kept the media in a frenzy while he considered to the possibility of running for the White House. Of course, it didn't hurt that his protracted decision-making process kept him in the public eye and, consequently, kept copies of his book flying off the bookshelves. In retrospect, I'm not so sure that General Powell was ever seriously thinking about running for the Oval Office, but rather about going to the bank. And General, I ain't mad at you! I'm never mad at a brother for getting paid.

But, needless to say, had Colin Powell decided to actually enter the race for the White House, it would have put Black America in a most interesting paradigm. Would Black voters have done the usual—supported the Democratic incumbent, in this case, Bill Clinton—or the unusual—supported a Black Republican? The only person who can really tell us the true answer to that question is Miss Dupree, and since she's not here this morning, we will move on. For countless reasons, my sense is that Black folks are growing more and more restless with the lack of real choices we have when we go to the polls.

I recall our dear friend Maxine Waters, the Chairwoman of the Congressional Black Caucus, saying back in 1992, after Bill Clinton selected Al Gore as his running mate, that Clinton/Gore would be the last time that she would support a ticket that had two White males at the top. My further sense is that in the coming months and years we are going to see many more so-called Black conservatives, although it still sounds like an oxymoron to me. But we are going to see more Black conservatives and more moderate Black Republicans of the Colin Powell/Jack Kemp stripe emerging as alternatives for Black voters who feel that the Democratic Party is taking us for granted now more than ever. While we may not be straight slaves on the Democratic plantation, many feel that we're not a step above being indentured servants and sharecroppers.

Our Republican friend, Cheryl Underwood, must be going crazy right now, loving this commentary. As you so clearly know, being a Republican, a member of the GOP, the Grand Old Party, ain't for me. I'd rather be *Hard Left* than half-right any day of the week. I've said before that we ought to quit using political terms like Left and Right, and start saying the Left and the half-Right because that's exactly what they are most often. Half-right. They give you half the facts, tell you half the story, show half the picture, tell you half the truth. Most of the time, they are half-right. But that's my opinion. Not to mention that I can't get with a party that still has not a single Black American, last time I checked, on its executive board. In 1997, the Republican National Committee said they wanted to reach out to Black folks while still having not a single Black on their executive board. So the GOP is not for me. If the question is whether I want to have (a) no one in the room (b) a Clarence Thomas disciple in the room, selling us out and doing the buck dance or (c) an African American in the room who has not forgotten that he is, in fact, an African American, then I, of course, choose (c).

Now, my time is out for the day, but on Thursday morning I want to tell you about a story that you heard first here on the *Tom Joyner Morning Show*. Thursday morning, I want to talk about a brother in Ohio, who happens to be the State Treasurer at the moment. His name is Ken Blackwell. I know we've got a whole lot of folks listening in Ohio this morning. He may very well be the next governor of Ohio. Behind Doug Wilder of Virginia, he would only be the second Black elected chief executor of a state in this country since Reconstruction. The hook is that Ken Blackwell is a Black Republican. On Thursday morning, we're going to talk about this brother named Ken Blackwell in Ohio. What his chances really are of becoming the next governor of the state of Ohio, and what kind of Black Republican—A, B, or C—is he going to be when he gets in the room?

Afterthought: *Ken Blackwell ultimately decided to run for Secretary of State in Ohio and not governor, at least not now.*

December 2, 1997

TJMS Topic: Life, Liberty, the Pursuit of Happiness *and* Healthcare for All!

There are literally, Tom, millions, in fact, tens of millions of Americans who are without healthcare coverage. I'd ask for a show of hands for those of you who don't have coverage, but I certainly don't want you taking your hands off the steering wheel with no coverage. So I'm not going to ask for a show of hands, but there are tens of millions of Americans who are without even basic fundamental healthcare coverage. Most are women and children, and most, of course, look just like us. Surprise, surprise!

President Clinton, you might recall, tried a few years ago, he and Hillary both, to push major health care reform legislation through Congress, which among other things would have guaranteed universal healthcare coverage for all Americans. You might also recall that the President and Hillary were handed their you-know-what on a platter, courtesy of a Republican-controlled Congress and a powerful healthcare industry lobby who said, "We don't think so." Over the past few weeks I've learned a little more than I care to know about healthcare, most fundamentally that being sick or injured ain't no joke. Thanks to the good natured but incessant teasing I received from Tom and the crew, most of you know by now that recently I had knee surgery for a torn lateral meniscus on my left knee.

Tom also just told you that while you were preparing to get your grub on last week for Thanksgiving, I was back in the hospital to have a cyst removed from my right vocal chord. Consequently, I was unable to eat, or more importantly to me, unable to talk for five days.

My throat hurt all during the Thanksgiving holiday. Have you ever noticed that the only folks who actually get these cysts and nodules on their vocal chords are the folks who use their voices to make a living? I haven't figured out why yet. My doctor is convinced that I contracted the cyst by repeatedly giving out the address for Peter Roth at *Fox* network and Patricia Hambrecht at Christie's one too many times. But I think it was worth it.

In any event, I was in Los Angeles a few weeks ago complaining and crying like a baby because I had just completed the knee surgery forty-eight hours prior, and was facing months of rehabilitation on my knee when I learned that throat surgery would be necessary on Thanksgiving Eve, of all days. Months of rehab, crutches, weight gain, throat surgery, no Thanksgiving with my family. I was singing the blues. "Nobody knows the trouble I've seen..." you know. I'm mostly singing the blues because...guess what? I do not have any healthcare insurance.

While I was driving down Wilshire Boulevard in L.A., complaining and crying like a baby, the Lord spoke to me. He said, "Tavis, I know you're not tripping. All this time I have blessed you. I have protected you. I have watched over you. I've kept you healthy so that you could perfect your passion and join the *Tom Joyner Morning Show* and join *BET*, knowing full well that if I'd allowed anything to happen to you just a year or two ago, you couldn't afford a Band-Aid let alone to have your knee reconstructed. And now, although it cost $12,000 for both procedures and rehab, now you can write a check for these procedures." And so I adjusted my attitude in a hurry. And at $12,000, I got a break! My excellent physicians, Dr. Barry Braiker, Dr. William Young and Dr. Madison Richardson, told me I was their friend and they liked watching and listening to me.

I got caught without healthcare coverage because I was in the midst of that ninety day pre-existing condition period, having just signed with a new provider. I had to wait ninety days. And it was during that very period that I learned that my knee had been blown out and that I needed throat surgery. So I had to come out-of-pocket. Now, my CPA tells me that I'll get all that money back next year at tax time, but that didn't help me when my physicians stuck out their hands *before* I went under anesthesia!

The bottom line is that we are still the only civilized nation in the world that does not offer basic, minimal, guaranteed healthcare coverage for its citizens, and that, I believe, is shameful. President Clinton indicated that he's going to make another attempt at healthcare reform again, and try to get, before he leaves office, some basic, fundamental healthcare coverage for all Americans. Universal healthcare coverage ought to be as guaranteed as life, liberty, and the pursuit of happiness. I was in a position at this point in my life to be able to afford what happened to me. But had it happened, as I said, a year or two ago, yours truly would have been in trouble.

Afterthought: *Yes, I now have health insurance, but the fight for universal healthcare coverage for all Americans must go on. So, more commentaries are scheduled to come on air.*

January 29, 1998

TJMS Topic: A "Vast Right-Wing Conspiracy"?

When we last spoke, I told you that a powerful chorus of voices was growing ever louder, echoing the sentiment that the right-wing was out to get the President and the First Lady by any means necessary. Little did I know that the very moment I was speaking those words to you, Hillary Rodham Clinton was appearing live on the *Today* show suggesting that a "vast right-wing conspiracy" was to blame for her husband's current and many of his past problems. The First Lady, as conservatives have argued over the past 48 hours, was playing the conspiracy card in a game of paranoid politics.

It is refreshing to know that someone other than Black folks believe in conspiracy theories. And just because you're paranoid doesn't mean somebody's not out to get you. Paranoiacs can and do have real enemies. But it is this word "conspiracy" that has the right-wing seeing red, and has sent them into overdrive making condescending and crass remarks dismissing the First Lady's comments. The word conspiracy does, for many, conjure up thoughts of Oliver Stone and *J.F.K.*, and sometimes, most especially on the Internet, these conspiracies do get a little out there. I'm just waiting for somebody to tell me that Humpty Dumpty was pushed off the wall, and didn't just have an accidental fall. You know Humpty was pushed!

As we Black folks know all too well, conspiracies do happen. The Tuskegee experiment, the CIA and crack cocaine in South Central L.A., and yesterday, Tom, on the way to the *Today* show, I heard you talking about the Scottsborough Boys. Let's put it this way, if the question is whether or not there is a concerted effort by the Right to bring down and embarrass the President and the First Lady, the answer in my mind is absolutely and unequivocally, yes. There is no question that this President and First Lady are the most maligned first couple ever to occupy the White House.

The politics practiced by the Right has a mean-spirited nature to it, what I call "politics in 3-D: Distortion, Deception and Dogmatism." When you have folks on the Right, even ministers of the Gospel like Jerry Falwell, telling folks on his television program, asserting that the President is guilty of murder, money laundering and drug peddling, that goes beyond the pale. And these folks have no shame about their behavior anymore. It used to be in politics you would throw a rock and hide your hand. Now these folks throw rocks and say, "Yeah, I did it. What of it?!" The Right is unabashed about saying that they are paying for Paula Jones's lawyers, her defense and for that makeover. Not even trying to act like they are not involved in the case. There is no shame in their game.

I've said all along that Bill Clinton is a public servant and not a perfect servant. He is not human and divine, he's just human. I sometimes get the sense that if Bill Clinton walked on water, some folks would ask why he didn't swim!

We have to do everything we can, Tom, finally, to protect the Office of the Presidency.

The so-called independent counsel, Kenneth Starr, said that his plot was foiled when the media broke this story. Starr's next step was to convince Monica Lewinsky to wear a wiretap and to go in to the presence of the President of the United States, the leader of the free world, and get the President on tape. Republican, Democrat, Tory or Whig, it doesn't matter. You've gone beyond the pale when you start talking about sending folks in the presence of the President of the United States to wiretap the President. That goes beyond Bill Clinton, I'm talking about protecting the institution of the Presidency. Kenneth Starr has gone too far.

About the Author

Tavis Smiley is the host of *BET Tonight with Tavis Smiley*, on Black Entertainment Television, political commentator for the *Tom Joyner Morning Show*, and appears regularly as a political analyst on CNN. He is the author of two books, *Just A Thought* and *Hard Left*. Tavis Smiley is single and lives in both Los Angeles and Washington D.C. In his spare time, Mr. Smiley enjoys a good game of *Scrabble* with friends.

Please send all correspondence for Tavis Smiley to: Tavis Smiley, 3870 Crenshaw Blvd., Suite 391, Los Angeles, CA 90008.

Publisher's Note

Partial proceeds from the sale of each book sold in 1998 will go to support the Tom Joyner Foundation's "Dollars For Scholars" program. This scholarship program is designed to support needy and deserving students who attend historically Black colleges and universities. For more information or to make a contribution call (900) 255-GIVE.

Special thanks to Glen Cooper, Dawn Fong, Carla Gonzales, Elizabeth Tesolin, the Beauty Girls, Laurie Williams, Tom Joyner and the entire *Tom Joyner Morning Show* staff, most especially Ross Alan and David Starr. And many thanks for the blessings of my family: Claude Pines, Maureen Foster Pines, Darryll Pines, Derek Pines and the Suttons.